AF675714

MEMORIES OF LOSS AND DREAMS OF PERFECTION

Unsuccessful Childhood Grieving and Adult Creativity

Delmont Morrison
Shirley Linden Morrison

Imagery and Human Development Series
Series Editor: Anees A. Sheikh

Routledge
Taylor & Francis Group
LONDON AND NEW YORK

First published 2016 by Baywood Publishing Company, Inc.

Published 2018 by Routledge
2 Park Square, Milton Park, Abingdon, Oxon OX14 4RN
52 Vanderbilt Avenue, New York, NY 10017

First issued in hardback 2018

Routledge is an imprint of the Taylor & Francis Group, an informa business

Copyright © 2016 by Taylor & Francis

All rights reserved. No part of this book may be reprinted or reproduced or utilised in any form or by any electronic, mechanical, or other means, now known or hereafter invented, including photocopying and recording, or in any information storage or retrieval system, without permission in writing from the publishers.

Notice:
Product or corporate names may be trademarks or registered trademarks, and are used only for identification and explanation without intent to infringe.

Library of Congress Catalog Number: 2005046540

Library of Congress Cataloging-in-Publication Data

Morrison, Delmont C., 1932-
Memories of loss and dreams of perfection : unsuccessful childhood grieving and adult creativity / Delmont Morrison, Shirley Linden Morrison.
p. cm. -- (Imagery and human development series)
Includes bibliographical references and index.
ISBN 0-89503-309-7 (cloth)
1. Grief in children. 2. Grief therapy. 3. Bereavement in children. 4. Loss (Psychology) in children. 5. Imagination in children. 6. Memory in children. 7. Authors--Psychology--Case studies. 8. Creative ability--Psychological aspects. 9. Creation (Literary, artistic, etc.)--Psychological aspects--Case studies. I. Morrison, Shirley Linden. II. Title. III. Series

BF723.G75M675 2005
155.9'37'083--dc22

2005046540

ISBN-13: 978-0-415-78607-2 (hbk)
ISBN-13: 978-0-89503-309-3 (pbk)

For our children,
Rebecca, Bruce, and Marielena
and our grandchildren,
Shannon, Shelby, Brendan, and Shirley

Contents

Introduction

EXPERIENCE AS IMAGINATION

Imagination as observed in make-believe and pretend play is the way experience is first represented in childhood thought. About the time toddlers can think about an object not in their view, they also show that the object is known in human terms. Piaget was observing the 21-month-old Jacqueline, when she saw a small shell and called it a cup and pretended to drink from it. Not long after that she saw the same shell and said "glass," "cup," and "hat," and incorporating the object into an event, it was a "boat in the water" (Piaget, 1962, p. 124). Objects in childhood imagination are seldom represented in isolation but most often in an event represented in action. Piaget's observations of Jacqueline at this time indicate that she animated her world with objects and events of her own creation and that she could be other people, such as her mother or grandmother. At about age four, Jacqueline created an imaginary creature: Aseau. At first Aseau was a bird, then later a dog, who helped her understand experience, provided moral authority when it was necessary to obey orders, and consolation when she was unhappy. This creature eventually evolved into an imaginary companion (Piaget, 1962, pp. 129-130).

Although the power of childhood imagination to structure experience in these human terms is modified over time, the human needs continue, and imagination, although modified and influenced by social awareness, continues to organize experience and memory of events with the egocentrisms of the individual. This book is a study of the enduring effect of childhood imagination. Relatively unaffected by the understanding of experience formed within the parameters of language and adult thought, and dominated by what Piaget described as preoperational thought, childhood imagination defines early experience in uniquely human and individual terms. Imagination at this time is flexible and can be used to organize experience in multiple sensory and egocentric dimensions. In the usual course of events, childhood imagination becomes more socialized and organized by less egocentric dimensions of thought and more stable, social interpersonal dimensions. However, the original richness of childhood imagination can still contribute to adult experience (Rosengren, Johnson, & Harris, 2000).

In this book we address an event in childhood that disrupts this developmental course, with the result that a child's imagination is restricted, yet in some ways intensely enriched, by memories of the past. Idiosyncratic in nature, these memories continue into adulthood. This childhood experience frequently results in clinical evaluation and interventions, and these procedures are used in this text as methods for studying imagination. The enduring effect of this early experience can also find expression in adult imagination. Under certain conditions, adults will use their memory for a creative reconstruction of this childhood experience. We use the lives and literary works of four authors to illustrate the profound effect of this childhood experience on adult imagination and creativity.

GRIEF AND MOURNING IN CHILDHOOD

A child's imagination can be significantly influenced by the death and emotional loss of a significant family member. The effect of this experience on the child's developing capacity for imagination and related cognitive functions, such as reflective thought, self-awareness, and memory of the event, will be greatly influenced by the family's reaction to the event and the child's experience of grief and mourning. The process of grieving and mourning in childhood is central to this book and is examined in detail in Chapters 1, 2, and 3.

The definitions of grief and mourning have evolved from observations of these two psychological processes in adults. *Grief,* as a reaction to loss, consists of feelings, physical sensations, cognitive responses, and behaviors. *Mourning* is the psychological process that accompanies grief, but involves the surviving individual's coming to terms with the immediate meaning of the loss and the future implications of life without the deceased. The successful result of this process is that the survivor understands the emotional and psychological meaning of the loss and believes that the future can have positive meaning. The psychoanalytic use of these two terms suggests that they are two interrelated yet separate processes. In successful mourning the survivor gets to the point that the memory of the lost individual is relinquished (Bowlby, 1960, p. 11) with the understanding that the loss is permanent and irreversible (Krueger, 1983, p. 590). With children and perhaps adults, clinical and casual observations indicate that affective components, such as sadness associated with loss and intense pleasurable memories of the lost individual, continue well after the event. These psychological processes can continue through childhood and into adulthood without associated indications of unsuccessful grieving or mourning. Another issue is that in children the process of mourning, and the degree the process involves cognitive as well as emotional factors, is significantly different from mourning in adults (Webb, 2002). The capacity of the five-year-old to understand death and loss in terms of both immediate comprehension and future anticipation is different cognitively and emotionally from that of a ten-year-old or a twenty-year-old. Grief reactions such as denial, anger, guilt, sadness, and longing for the deceased are common in children. Childhood grief occurs, but mourning—in the sense that a more personally satisfying and socially congruent conclusion about the meaning of the loss is achieved—is a longer process. The child's mourning process is characterized by continuing strong, emotional feelings about the lost individual as well as compensatory fantasies and conclusions about that individual. For example, the child may anticipate that the deceased will come back, may believe the dead person's spirit is actually present, or will rigidly maintain certain behaviors that the lost person would appreciate and approve of. The fantasy component of the mourning process is normal in a child and represents the child's continuing emotional attachment to the deceased (Klass, Silverman, & Nickman, 1996).

Children experience grief and mourning differently from adults because of their different cognitive capacities and a limited capacity to tolerate emotional pain. Their difficulties in verbalizing their feeling and their sensitivity to the views of their peers may also interfere with their personal understanding of death and loss. These factors contribute to their experience of the mourning process and indicate that a non-conflicted and personally satisfying understanding of the meaning of the loss of the loved individual, which is an indication of successful mourning, will usually take more time in children than in the adolescent or adult. Grieving and mourning are psychologically inseparable processes in childhood. The cognitive awareness of the functional independence of affect and thought, and the more complicated awareness of the interaction of the two, is a gradual developmental process that is not achieved until roughly age eight to twelve (Fast, 1985, Chap. 5). Because of the continuing influence of the emotions of grieving on mourning, the two terms are used interchangeably in this text. This is important because one of the significant components of unsuccessful grieving is that the negative affects toward the deceased that existed prior to the death often do not find expression in memory and are never completely integrated into the child's understanding of the meaning of the loss. In this situation, a more complete understanding of the meaning of the death and loss of the deceased is never accomplished. It is the child who has ambivalent conflicted feelings toward the deceased who is at risk for unsuccessful grieving and mourning.

For this child, the immediate results of unsuccessful grieving and mourning are anxiety and depressing preoccupations regarding the lost individual that reflect the intense yet unintegrated feelings of both affection and dislike that existed before the death. The existing fantasies that accompany either the feelings of affection or the dislike may be incongruous with the child's perception of the reactions of psychologically important members of the family. This internal and interpersonal tension can result in a significant compromise in the child's cognitive and emotional development.

THREE STABLE SYSTEMS OF THOUGHT

In the context of this book, the child is understood as evolving from a developmental stage characterized by a lack of differentiation between self and others to a stage where this differentiation is a stable, cognitive function. This psychological development is not automatic and is stimulated by the child's experience, as discussed in Chapters 1 and 2. These chapters outline the necessary interactions between the child and immediate caregivers that are the basis for the child's evolving capacity to be aware of the emotional and cognitive dimensions of self in the context of an awareness of similar processes in other people. This developmental process requires three interrelated stable cognitive structures: 1) Representational thought, 2) reflective thought, and 3) autonomous thought (Noy, 1979). Unsuccessful grieving in childhood disrupts the development of these cognitive functions and the differentiation of self. It is important to understand how the child first structures and forms memories of experience without the organizational influence of these stable, cognitive systems. Prior to development of these systems, the child in the undifferentiated stage consistently demonstrates a lack of discrimination between what has been described as "me" and "not me" (Winnicott, 1965). This normally occurring developmental stage is characterized by understanding being established through transitional interactions that serve to extend the domain of self. Transitional objects, imaginary companions, pretending to be a desirable person, and, at a later stage, paracosmic play all function to reduce the child's growing awareness of the boundaries and limitation of self. Although this early use of imagination is normal, the first five chapters demonstrate how this transitional thinking can be used defensively in unsuccessful grieving.

Representational thought structures an experience and the memory of that experience through images and symbols. Initially, the representational systems of the child are unstable and idiosyncratic. With the development of language, and what Piaget (1954) described as operational thought, and the socialization process, these images and symbols become more stable and less idiosyncratic. Closely related to representational thought is reflective thought. Before the development of reflective thought, the child's representations of events are immediate. Reflective thought represents the capacity of the child to organize knowledge of an event by observing his or her internal experience of that event. Autonomous thought is observed when the child can consciously manipulate the images and symbols of experience and the memory of experience.

Early experience occurs with the dominating effect of an imagination that is not limited by these later-developing three stable systems of thought. Awareness of self and others is an acquired cognitive capacity that is greatly determined by the child's experience with objects that are both social and non-social in nature. In either case, over time the child's understanding reflects a growing awareness of dimensions of experience such as cause and effect, time, object permanency, and the interaction of such concepts, as well as an awareness of the internal experience of interpersonal relationships. A major characteristic of early childhood thought is that all this experience is initially organized by the influence of the imagination of the egocentric child. Between the ages of approximately two and eight, while the child is discovering the boundaries and limitations of self, imagination functions to synthesize various aspects of the child's experience. Reflective thought obtains more influence in the latter part of this age range. A number of events will influence the development of the child's capacity to structure and to integrate experience with an imagination modulated by reflective thought and a growing awareness of self and others. These important organizers of the child's understanding of early experience have been observed by Piaget (1954), Bowlby (1969), Winnicott (1965), and Fast (1985). There are also a number of events in early experience that can contribute to the development of limitations in imagination and disruption in the awareness of self and others (Pine, 1985). This book addresses a particular event: early loss and unsuccessful grieving that can compromise the development of the three stable cognitive systems and the development of self-awareness. The total effect of the experience of early loss is best understood in the context of the child's family.

LOSS AND THE FAMILY

Generally, children do not experience the traumatic stress associated with death in their lives and therefore they do not think much about it. Children think about aspects of their most immediate experience and typically in narcissistic dimensions. Although they may obtain some awareness of death through a friend's experience, the media, or, more personally, the loss of a loved pet, the emotions of death, grief, and mourning are unknown to them. This is supported by the general tendency of parents and other adult family members to avoid the issues of death, because of their own emotional reaction to this universal, yet psychologically threatening experience. There are developmental, cognitive factors that will influence the child's progression to the final knowledge that death is irreversible, inevitable, and universal. It is assumed that this conclusion is made by the time the child is approximately seven or eight years of age, but clinical observations indicate that the child's individual experiences with death can influence both the cognitive and emotional understanding of the event (Webb, 2002, Chap. 1). The crucial psychological processes that contribute to both the cognitive and emotional reactions are found in the context of the child's evolving understanding and awareness of self in the family. This psychological process is examined in Chapters 2, 3, and 4.

The important element in grieving and mourning is that there has been a relationship with a person that is valued, and death results in the irreversible termination of that relationship. The child feels deprived by the loss. When the lost person has been the object of mostly positive feelings, the grieving process involves the profound experience of losing a loved individual. When the child has ambivalent feelings toward the deceased, the issues are more complex. In either situation, the degree of congruency between the family's reaction and the child's reaction is crucial in terms of the outcome of grieving and, eventually, mourning. Chapter 2 deals with the grieving process in the child whose feelings about the deceased are ambivalent and incongruent with the feelings of important family members. The child's growing capacity for reflective thought results in an initially inarticulate awareness of motivations of simultaneous love and dislike, competitive feelings, jealousy, and the wish that the deceased was absent. This cognitive awareness evolves within the family system and the wish of the child to have his or her emotional needs for love and security fulfilled in that system. In this interpersonal context, the child may be angry at the same person he or she depends upon, such as a parent or older sibling. This results in ambivalent feelings that have their source in the child's internal and interpersonal experience. The child's developing cognitive capacity to recognize and own these psychological states generates internal stress. With the stress of the death and loss of an important family member, the conflicted relationship in the family may be further agitated, with the result that the child's needs are not recognized or met by the family.

THE UNCONSCIOUS

In a situation such as that just described, the child's growing conscious awareness of his or her negative motives and fantasies regarding the deceased and the grieving family members becomes a cognitive signal for anxiety. Unacceptable wishes toward key family members can no longer be explored in the domain of conscious thought, and a new, unconscious cognitive system for reducing anxiety through defense mechanisms is developed. A frequent defense mechanism evolving from this psychological state is the child's identification with the idealized lost parent or sibling. Under these conditions successful grieving does not occur, because the mourning process is dominated by defensive fantasies that are protective of self. Although anxiety is reduced, the child does not develop an understanding of his or her full range of feelings toward the deceased and key members of the family, or an understanding of the meaning of the loss. Grieving as an emotional process, and mourning as a cognitive process involving memory, remain undifferentiated.

Chapter 5 examines the long-term effect of unsuccessful grieving in adulthood. These unresolved childhood conflicts find expression in an adult who searches for relationships with idealized individuals as a means of resolving his or her own feelings of low self-esteem. The sense of being psychologically incomplete can be momentarily reduced in romantic relationships that seldom endure. The continued development of representational and reflective thought and sense of self is disrupted in various ways, as we will discuss. Because of these early conflicts, the development of autonomous thought is compromised. Imagination is limited and memory is over-determined by enduring concerns about death and loss.

UNDERSTANDING LOSS: PLAY THERAPY

Chapters 3 and 4 explore the immediate effects of unsuccessful grieving on the child. A child's first experience with death through the loss of a beloved pet, and the effect of this experience on the child's imagination, is illustrated in the content of a child's play. In our case story, we explore the importance of the family in helping the child, Benny, cope with the loss of his pet dog, Dusty. This case demonstrates the details of play therapy in helping this six-year-old deal with the emotional loss of his parents, who were in the middle of a hostile divorce, as well as the loss of Dusty, who was a source of comfort and identification for this lonely, isolated boy. We discuss clinical issues in evaluating and treating bereaved children and their families (Webb, 2002) with a special focus on the importance of trauma as a major contributing factor in both evaluation and treatment (Cohen et al., 2002). In this text, unsuccessful grieving is viewed as related to the child's development of defense mechanisms to reduce the anxiety generated by death and loss. Play therapy demonstrates this process and is presented as an intervention to reduce anxiety and the use of psychological defenses. The major goals in this therapeutic approach are to help the child develop reflective thought in the context of a trusting relationship. This treatment is illustrated in the case story of the eight-year-old Tyrone. Tyrone was raised with Lucas, his half brother, who was his senior by four years. Lucas was an outstanding basketball player, and the boys' way of relating was through playing basketball. Tyrone both admired and disliked this father-like figure. When Lucas died by drowning, Tyrone's unsuccessful grieving reaction included depression, seeing the spirit of Lucas, and idealizing his lost sibling in the context of an inability to explore his more negative feelings toward Lucas and his mother. Play therapy consisted of a pretend basketball game in which Tyrone began to understand his complex feelings toward Lucas. The case stories of Benny and Tyrone demonstrate the importance and the complications of working with a child's parents.

UNRESOLVED MOURNING AND ADULT IMAGINATION

Unsuccessful grieving in childhood has long-lasting effects that are expressed in the adult. These effects are outlined in Chapter 5. The development of defense mechanisms in childhood disrupts the normal development of representational, reflective, and autonomous thought. The consequences of this for adults' capacity to maintain relationships is significant. Cognitively limited in the awareness and understanding of their own inner states, they have difficulties understanding motivations and psychological states in other people. This is a significant limitation in intimate relationships. Identification of the other with the idealized memory of the lost family member is supported by the lack of a real relationship with that person. The consequent false sense of self is associated with a sense of emotional incompleteness. The attempt to mitigate this state is often the basis for entering into intimate relationships. The person who is loved is essentially created from need and cannot be known beyond the memories of the past loss of love. Dominated by their emotions and imagination, such individuals are limited in their capacity for reciprocity in relationships.

EARLY LOSS AND ADULT CREATIVITY

Within the limits of childhood imagination and experiences, a child's successful grieving and mourning results in an understanding and mastery of this universal and mysterious event. Accomplished within the limits of childhood thought, this understanding can evolve into the more mature comprehension of the experience in adulthood. Unsuccessful grieving in childhood results in the egocentric conclusion commonly found in the thinking of a child. Consequently, a more socially shared conclusion does not evolve, and understanding and mastery fail to develop. The attempt at mastery becomes an adult preoccupation. For the child, the attempts to understand will be expressed by imagination in dreams, drawings, and play. If these activities occur in the context of a relationship that provides insight for the child into his or her own poorly understood motivations, mastery and understanding can occur. For the creative adult, these same preoccupations with early loss can be expressed in imagination by telling stories and writing. The stories often have themes reflecting a nostalgia and idealization of the experienced death. A tremendous emotional charge associated with death is also expressed, and the relationships described in the stories are often based on attempts to control and master death. Chapter 5 and the following four chapters explore this view of the source of creativity in the lives of four authors: Emily Brontë, J. M. Barrie, Isak Dinesen, and Jack Kerouac. These four writers of loss all experienced the death of significant family members during their childhood. The effect of this experience, along with their unsuccessful grieving and mourning, is seen in their adult lives and their most significant poems and novels.

Although the case is made for an association between early loss, unsuccessful grieving, and later creativity, it is clear that creativity is a complex process that cannot be adequately explained by this one event. The relationship between the experience of early loss in childhood and creativity has been noted previously by behavioral scientists interested in creativity (Pollack, 1978). However, an association with unsuccessful grieving has not been made. The source of adult creativity is based on multiple factors that may find expression in different domains of creativity (Sternberg, 1999). But the link between the richness of early childhood imagination (Singer & Singer, 1990) and its continuing expression in adult creativity may be partially explained by the psychologically significant event in childhood of never having the opportunity to grieve and mourn and, eventually, to understand the meaning of loss.

CHAPTER 1

First Ways of Knowing

> . . . huge and mighty forms that do not live
> like living men, moved slowly through my mind.
> By day, and were the trouble of my dreams.
>
> Wordsworth, *The Prelude*

This book explores the development and uses of imagination and reflective thought and a particular early experience that can influence this development. As these two uniquely human ways of organizing early experience develop and interact, the individual's comprehension of experience and self evolves. All the child's experience will influence this process, but clearly the most influential are the early and enduring interactions with those intimate caregivers and loved ones who constitute that child's family. One event occurring in the child's early family experience can have a profound influence on the development of the child's imagination, reflective thought, and sense of self: early loss and unsuccessful grieving.

This text examines in detail the complications of unsuccessful grieving for the child, with the conclusion that the development of imagination, reflective thought, and eventually memory is formed, and in some ways frozen in time, by the individual's chronic preoccupation with the meaning of death and loss. Children tell their story of this experience in pretend play. For adults, the same experiences are the source of the major themes in their thoughts about themselves and their intimate relationships. Creative adults construct a memory of loss and use their imagination to tell their story, just as the child uses imagination to tell a similar story in play. The common theme is mastery of the early experience of death and loss through compensatory imagination that limits reflective thought but protects a fragile and false sense of self.

We will examine the immediate effects on imagination of unsuccessful grieving in the play therapy of the eight-year-old Tyrone, who had just experienced the death of his older half-brother (Chapter 4). The long-term effects of unsuccessful grieving on imagination and memory are illustrated in the lives and literary works of four authors who experienced loss during childhood: Emily Brontë, J. M. Barrie, Isak Dinesen, and Jack Kerouac (Chapters 5 to 8).

IMAGINATION AND EXPERIENCE

The development of the child's early experiences with and knowledge of objects is significant (Mullen, 1995; Sparrow et al., 1984). At about five to eight months, an infant girl will bang a small spoon on the table and may put it in her mouth. If the spoon is taken away, she most likely will protest and clearly show that she wants it back. However, if the spoon is slowly moved across the table before her eyes and then dropped over the edge so that it disappears from her sight, she will turn her eyes away to the next most interesting event. Once the spoon is out of her sight it does not exist. A short time later, at nine to twelve months, if the same sequence is repeated she will look over the table edge in pursuit of the disappearing spoon. At about the same age, she will take great pleasure in throwing the spoon in order to make it disappear. This activity is greatly enhanced in terms of the infant's obvious pleasure if a nearby adult consistently brings the spoon back for another throw. The infant is actively engaged now in controlling the appearance and disappearance of objects in an interpersonal context.

During this time, the same spoon can be taken from her and slowly moved as she watches it disappear under a napkin. Although the infant will look for the spoon if it disappears off the table, as it disappears under the napkin she will again direct her attention to a more interesting event. However, just a short six months or so later she will reach for the napkin and, upon removing it, smile with satisfaction and retrieve the spoon. In this brief interval, she demonstrates progressive development in the knowledge that the spoon exists beyond her perception. However, at the same age, if the spoon is hidden under the same napkin and secretly moved under a napkin near it, she will remove the first napkin but not continue the search—even as she seems surprised that the spoon is missing. Given the same experience at 20 months, she will now go immediately to the next napkin and find the spoon. Observations indicate that at 12 months, the spoon existed as a function of her last action and she would only search for it where she last found it; now, at 20 months, the spoon exists as a permanent object, requiring that she modify her perceptions and actions to have any control over it. She can think about the absent spoon and make conclusions. It is significant that at about the same time this awareness develops, using her imagination the child demonstrates an opposite conclusion about the existence of the spoon. She can use it to pretend to feed her doll, and she can, with a willing mother, pretend to feed the mother who has fed her. Now the spoon exists as a permanent object that is controlled and defined by her imagination.

At age 16 to 24 months, the child can think about an object or person that is not present. Examples of this process demonstrate that image formation is not passive but active. Parents have left their 16-month-old son with a babysitter.

They tell the boy that they will be back soon, then they leave by a door leading to steps that go up a small hill. The boy watches them leave and go up the steps. He is comfortable with the familiar babysitter and they start to play. However, an hour after the parents have left, the boy falls while running and bumps his head. The babysitter tries to comfort him, but he runs to the door and, looking outside to the steps, calls for his "dada" and "mama." He evokes the image of his parents, who represent comfort. The same boy eight months later plays with the babysitter pretending to drive a toy truck, making the sounds of a honking horn and the sounds of the engine. When the parents return to take him home in their car, he climbs into the father's lap in the car and, grabbing the steering wheel, honking the horn, and making the sound of the engine, pretends to drive the car.

This tremendous growth in awareness of self and experience takes place in about 24 months and illustrates two major characteristics of childhood thought that continues through the life span. Ways of knowing expand by the child's interactions in events. Understanding of the outcomes of these interactions is organized by representations that correspond to the more objective qualities of experience, resulting in logical, sequential, and paradigmatic conclusions. However, at the same time, understanding of these interactions is organized by imagination that consistently produces conclusions that are often juxtaposed and in contrast to objective thought. These conclusions are nurtured by subjective wishes. The two modes of understanding are in constant interaction. But a child's understanding of interpersonal relationships is often fueled by the subjective wish, and the influence of this development on the organization of early experience is the focus of what follows.

THE POSSIBILITIES OF EXPERIENCE

The examples of the girl pretending to feed the mother who had fed her, and the boy pretending to drive the car like his father, illustrate two important aspects of childhood imagination. The child can pretend to be like someone else and to have that person's ability and thereby extend and construct experience to fulfill a wish. The best examples of childhood imagination are seen in pretend play between ages three and eight years (Singer & Singer, 1990). There is evidence that children at this time are developing knowledge of experience that corresponds to the more socially accepted and stable objective conclusions. These stable objective conclusions are dependent on cognitive concepts that correspond to the external structure of events involving object constancy, constancy of space, and causality and temporal relationships (Gopnik & Meltzoff, 1998; Piaget, 1954). Initially, these concepts are unstable, and the child's interpretation of events is variable and inaccurate. Eventually these concepts become more stable and are integrated into other constructs, with the result that between ages eight and twelve the child has an accurate system of interpretation for the occurrence of these external events.

During the interval between ages two and eight, however, imagination is not dominated by this new information and new way of thinking. Imagination is organized by wish and subjective conclusions that are noteworthy by their constant shift in focus. Imagination is not greatly influenced by the restrictions of more realistic constructs, and the child can pretend to be like almost anything. At about ages two to three, when the child demonstrates the capacity to represent objects and events not present, he or she can use a broad range of objects to represent that object in an imagined event. A short stick can represent an airplane or a rocket arching above the ground, having a story constructed by the child. Social concepts, logic, and discrimination between animate and inanimate objects are not determined by conventional thought but by imagination. One object or gesture can be substituted for another. A child can identify with a horse by pretending to be a horse by tossing her hair, prancing, and neighing, while her companion can pretend to be the horse trainer by putting a string around the horse's neck and holding a stick in an authoritarian manner. The capacity to be the same as something or someone else and to make something the same as something else is the beginning of identification and metaphor construction. Both are used increasingly as play becomes organized and is used to create a story of events and construct a memory of an event. As play becomes organized, it tells stories about past, present, and future events. Imagination expressed as stories in play serves to create a subjective understanding and mastery of the child's interaction in events over the total time span. Memory is constructed by subjective imagination. This imaginative understanding is accompanied by the growing capacity to understand events based on conclusions organized by stable concepts about external events, occurring in natural and social contexts. This growth in awareness results in more consistency in the child's thought and increasingly produces a limitation on the boundaries of imagination. Although the child's increasing awareness and use of objective socialized thought produces significant shifts in the use of imagination, it does not necessarily limit the child's capacity to use imagination.

IMAGINING THE SELF

As the infant and toddler initially encounter events, the experience occurs without the contribution of the awareness of a self. The self is discovered over time, and a conscious awareness grows of the contribution of the self in organizing experiences. Prior to an articulated awareness of self, experience is organized by the child's egocentric thought, without the significant modulation of an awareness of the contribution of egocentric thought (Fast, 1985). The most significant cognitive factor in modifying this process is reflective thought: the capacity to experience self. The details of this experience for the cognitive development of the child have been described in detail by Piaget (1954), and for the development of emotional and interpersonal relationships by Fonagy and Moran (1991) and Noam (1988).

This discrimination and differentiation regarding self and external events begins at about age two, as the child demonstrates a capacity to think about absent people and events and has a memory of such events. At this time the child also demonstrates imitation and identification, indicating some awareness that people exist independent of himself or herself. This marks the beginning evolution of how a child organizes experiences. Events are initially experienced in undifferentiated global terms in which thought and references are not distinguished and thought is organized without an accurate awareness of external processes such as time, causality, and object constancy. With the gradual development of stable cognitive structures and an articulate self-awareness, events are organized by being the subject of reflective-socialized thought. Thought and action eventually become differentiated, and events are no longer uncritically taken as real but instead can be referred to increasingly complex concepts, including the self, that contribute to the understanding of experience. The early ways of knowing do not disappear. In the normal course of development, the first memories formed by the early ways of knowing organized by self-centered egocentric thought are modified and integrated into the evolving sense of self.

This phase of cognitive development, occurring roughly between the ages of two and eight, has a profound influence on the child's ability to adapt to and incorporate socialized systems of thought. With the development of reflective thought the child eventually comes to an understanding that other people are in some ways both like and unlike the self and that others are responsive in a social system that assumes this understanding and consequent expectations. This awareness of self and others appears to develop in stages of complexity, from the child's initial awareness that the goals and self-interest of others may be separate from his or her own goals and self-interest, to a later stage, where the individual accepts relationships by understanding the perspective of others and is not governed only by self-interest.

The development of reflective thought and the awareness of the psychological states of others is complex but appears to be present in two- to three-year-old children. Three-year-old children have some capacity to understand that other people have feelings and intentions different from their own, and they can demonstrate this understanding in their interactions with other children (Butterworth et al., 1991). It is significant that the awareness of self and others corresponds to the development of another indicator of socialized thought: language. Memories formed before the beginning of self-differentiation are mostly idiosyncratic and non-verbal, organized by sensory images and evocative emotional states. The process of self-differentiation results in the child's gradual discrimination that events understood by the first ways of knowing are different from the later occurring systems of knowing. This is a gradual process. For a considerable time, imagination allows the child to continue to organize past, present, and future experiences by a combination of idiosyncratic and socialized systems. As demonstrated in the play of children between the ages of three and eight, a child can imagine multiple personas for himself or herself and for others. Although the child is developing a sense of self and an awareness of others, because of egocentrism the child's awareness of others is functionally dominated by his or her own perspective and wish. The understanding of relationships is based on knowledge acquired from interpersonal interactions, which is a life-long learning process. The important issue in early development is that the transformations in the cognitive states of the awareness of self and others take place.

Experience of events that generate anxiety and serve as a threat to a developing sense of self can significantly affect the child's use of imagination by limiting it to compensatory themes that are repetitive attempts to understand and master the past. In the experience of early loss, the child has an initial interpretation of the event that is incongruous with that of other family members. This conflict dominates the child's imagination and sense of self. In unsuccessful grieving this conflict becomes internalized and can be an enduring and dominant part of the personality. When this child plays, the identifications made and the stories told are limited by confusing preoccupations and tensions that have no resolution. The play is repetitious. The metaphors used in this play reflect an effort to understand and master that is accompanied by prevailing themes of guilt and depression. All this results in unsatisfactory conclusions, because the images and themes in play generate anxiety rather than reduce it. If these conflicts are not resolved, over time the child moves into an adolescence and adulthood where a memory is constructed to provide some cohesion to what is experienced as a fragmented history. The preoccupations with death and loss limit imagination and memory and over-determine the individual's sense of self and relationships. Representational thought regarding the loss is characterized by disturbing, affect-laden images and metaphors, while reflective thought becomes restrictive and protective of self, and because of the interaction of these two systems, autonomous thought is compromised.

The child in these stressful circumstances finds no inner satisfaction with his or her morbid thoughts, and interpersonal experience offers limited satisfaction. Because of guilt and depression such children may not wish to leave their room or house. At school, they may over-react to another child's teasing or a teacher's effort to correct a poorly organized classroom project. They may become very aggressive and have behavior problems at school and at home. Disturbing dreams and night terrors are common (Cain et al., 1964; Cohen et al., 2002). These behaviors often bring the child to the attention of a clinician. This was the case for Tyrone, who was seen in play therapy following the accidental death of his older half-brother, Lucas. Tyrone's experience of unsuccessful grieving and his identification with the lost and idealized Lucas are discussed more fully in Chapter 4. Among other things, Tyrone's case demonstrates the unified effort of the family to construct a memory of the lost person in idealized terms.

With time, the individual's habitual use of imagination for self-protection and compensation structures the memory of the past event, and a personal myth is created. Although imagination is restricted in terms of content, the content itself is emotionally charged. This process has been a source of creativity for some individuals.

MEMORY AND CREATIVITY

The child preoccupied with the unresolved conflicts of early loss has a limited range of interpretations of past experience and future expectations. Because of the limits of imagination, the past intrudes and experience is repeated. In the adult there is an enduring depression with a sense of an unfulfilled self and a chronic lack of connection with immediate experience. This central core of personality can be momentarily altered by relationships that for a time provide a different and more positive definition of self. In an interrelated process of retelling the story of death and loss in different metaphors, the storyteller creates a sense of mastery and a different, more positive sense of self. When these writers of loss face the blank page to begin the creative process, their effort to create will be over-determined and, as in the grieving child's play, there will be a repetition of themes and desired conclusions that do not correspond to actual experience. Like the themes in the play of a child who has experienced unsuccessful grieving, the imagination of these authors is both limited and enriched by their histories. Like the grieving child they tell stories that can be understood in terms of their history of early loss and chronic grieving. Because of their talent these writers may not be limited by these preoccupations and they can tell other stories. This applies to a limited number of creative individuals, and there are many writers who do not share such histories, psychological make-up, or motivation yet are recognized for their creativity. However, generally, the stories they tell will differ from those of the authors discussed here. Stories told by these writers of loss are often inspired by intense and enduring memories and romantic relationships, both real and imagined. The unresolved pain and confusion of early loss result in an identification with the idealized image of the lost individual and in a psychology of romantic ideation that determines the individual's adult relationships. This nostalgia for death and early loss is a major source of creative imagination and the motivation to create. There are four authors who may best demonstrate this source of creativity. They lived and loved at very different times, and represent more than 151 years of cultural and social change that influenced their creativity. The experience of the early loss of love and the wish to retell that story in terms of romantic ideation unite Emily Brontë, J. M. Barrie, Isak Dinesen, and Jack Kerouac. These writers tell us that the mystery of death and the pain of loss can best be understood by imagination.

CHILDHOOD AND CREATIVITY

The sources of creative expression in adulthood are many, but certainly one of the most imaginative periods of human experience is during childhood, and the period of childhood has been considered a source for later creative thought (Morrison, 1988; Singer & Singer, 1990). Early childhood thought gains some importance in the development of imagination because it is the first way experience and memories are organized. The first way of knowing occurs in the context of idiosyncratic thought peculiar to childhood, during a time when the development of reflective thought and knowledge of self is just starting. Beginning with representational thought at age two and extending roughly to age six and eight, the child's cognitive organization is preverbal rather than verbal and egocentric rather than logical (Santostefano, 1988), with both positive and negative affect determining the child's conception and memory of experience. Over time, the child's organization of experience becomes more social and influenced by language, but it is assumed that the original ways of knowing remain an important influence throughout life (Noy, 1979) and contribute to creativity in adulthood (Gardner, 1983).

The nature of the child's first representations of experience is unique and contributes directly to creative thought. There is a perpetual confusion between subjective and more objective views of the world, with the child's subjective frame of reference greatly determining the interpretation of events. Unconscious of their own motivations, children conclude that it is the power of their own wish or will that determines the outcome of events. Thus magical thinking dominates a child's experience and conclusions about causality for both non-personal and interpersonal events. The child's conclusion that inanimate and animate objects are influenced by his or her own wish and that inanimate objects have humane characteristics both enriches and distorts the child's interpretation of the world. As four-year-olds observe the moon move in the same direction as they walk, both egocentrism and narcissism contribute to their conclusion that the moon is following them (Piaget, 1962). J. M. Barrie never lost this capacity to organize experience as children do. He used his imagination to create a lasting image of egocentrism and narcissism in Peter Pan, a boy dominated by one wish—to never grow up—who lives in a magical world of Neverland. The use of the word *Neverland* by Barrie indicates his knowledge that this is a temporary place.

During childhood the world is in the process of being known through the interaction of the child's egocentric thought with both personal and impersonal objects that requires a sorting out of objects as "me" or "not me." Initially, the child's inner state dominates, and objects are understood in the subjective terms of the child's needs and imagination. Inanimate objects having some association with human characteristics such as being soft and warm or smelling like the child or the mother will be a source of comfort when present and a signal for anxiety when absent. The panic when the object is not available illustrates the need for control. Transitional objects (Winnicott, 1965) serve as a means of maintaining the child's need for security and fantasy of control as the discrimination between subjective self and experience develops. Fantasies about transitional objects develop early and illustrate the power of childhood imagination. By extending the child's will, imagination works to reduce the tension generated by the awareness that events function in ways that demand the development of more accommodative means of knowing the world—especially those individuals who make up that part of the world that loves and cares for the child.

Numerous fantasies function to support the child's more egocentric ways of knowing (Singer & Singer, 1990). The capacity to pretend demonstrates the beginning of a child's awareness of self and the existence of other people and other ways of knowing and doing. However, pretend play is often accompanied by the creation of a subjective wished-for state or an imaginary friend and companion that serve various functions (Taylor, 1999). Like the transitional object, the imaginary friend extends the child's will, but at a more complex level the child's imagination often creates an alter ego having characteristics that the creator feels he or she lacks. Closely linked to this compensatory function of imagination is identification with known individuals. These may be individuals within the family, but can be known in a larger social reference, such as figures from television or the movies. This level of identification takes place as the child's developing concept of self becomes more evaluative and, in compensation, the child imagines what it would be like to be someone else or to possess a desirable someone. These fantasies mark the beginning of romantic ideation. Following the death of his brother, Jack Kerouac at age five developed an imaginary friend who was maintained with a few modifications into adulthood. This fantasy eventually expressed itself in Kerouac's friendship with William Burroughs and in his novel, *Dr. Sax*.

METAPHORS AND THE EXTENSION OF SELF

Childhood thought is dominated by wish and organized at first by metaphors of actions, symbol, and language (Santostefano, 1988). The meaning of a child's experience is structured by knowing a new event or person in terms of properties that belong to something else or someone else experienced in the past. The child perceives a shared attribute by comparing the new event with a memory. The younger child will often represent this process in images, action, and symbols. For example, a four-year-old girl sees real horses for the first time in a parade, and later is seen portraying the maternal qualities of horses by pretending she is a horse that is protective and loving. Her horse likes little girls and wants to give them rides wherever they would like to go. During the parade the little girl was frightened of the horses, did not want to look at them, and clung to her mother. In this example the child, seeing something new and frightening, was able to reduce the anxiety by identification and by metaphorically transferring the meaning of the experience into something known and controllable. As the girl develops language, she may verbally express her unique view of horses, such as reading about them or telling stories reflecting the strong gentle qualities of horses or images of horses such as unicorns. It is important to note that the original metaphors were represented by actions and images, and later by language. As an adult, the memory of an event in the past may consist of metaphors of action, images, and language, and when these metaphors are combined with affects such as happiness or anxiety the memories can take an enduring place in personality.

Metaphorical thinking is a further elaboration of childhood thought expressed in transitional objects. External objects and events are known by the child predominately in terms of internal states and needs. The compensatory capacity of childhood thought is seen when the closeness of a familiar soft blanket or favorite doll provides comfort to the child. This occurs because the objects are concrete representations of a memory of the original comforting object, the mother, not immediately available or under the child's control. The transitional object is possibly one of the first metaphors for lost narcissistic love. Metaphors formed in childhood to represent emotional events experienced during that time endure, and when explored by the imagination of a poet produce the shared emotional experience that is art. This effort to establish the metaphorical "truth" of early experience can occur over an extended period of time during which the artist constructs new metaphors to represent the original meanings. Wordsworth is an example of a poet who felt that his childhood memories were the basis of his creative imagination and that these memories were greatly influenced by nature. For approximately 50 years, Wordsworth wrote and revised sections of his autobiographical poem *The Prelude* (1805). For Wordsworth, as for Isak Dinesen, there was an intimate communication between man and nature that inspires and serves the creative act. In essence, the poet makes nature known and understandable in human terms, and through metaphorical image nature is made a symbol representing human experience and emotions. This is seen in the section of *The Prelude* in which Wordsworth describes an actual boyhood episode in which he steals a boat on a lake at night. He rowed away in the stolen boat:

> When from behind that craggy Steep, till then
> The bound of the horizon, a huge Cliff,
> As if with voluntary power instinct,
> Upreared its head: I struck and struck again
> And, growing still in stature, the huge cliff
> Rose up between me and the stars, and still,
> With measured motion, like a living thing,
> Strode after me (p. 12).

The mountain's shadow becomes the representation of boyhood guilt, and animated by this human emotion it pursues the small boy in his boat. Thus in imagination all nature becomes involved in this childhood act of piracy, forgotten by this time by everyone except Wordsworth.

The capacity to organize experiences and memory based on emotional states such as guilt, illustrated numerous times in the metaphors of Wordsworth's poetry, contributes to the richness of childhood imagination but also indicates the socialization of thought. The egocentric nature of early childhood thought is universal, but the unique affective components such as love and hate, eroticism and aggression, pride and guilt, are uniquely acquired by each individual child in intimate interactions with those who are emotionally close. This combination of egocentrism, with the fusion between subjective emotional needs and external experience, and structuring and knowing experiences through psychological tension has profound meaning for the development of imagination and creativity. This first way of knowing results in a dynamic interplay between egocentric wishes and socialized thought that generates a psychological space between the conclusions of wish and reality. Although developed in childhood, this tension between the satisfactions of the alternative conclusions available between wish and reality continues with everyone into adulthood. For some, exploring and expressing the meaning of this tension through the written word contributes to the creativity of the poet and writer.

The motivation to explore and provide a conclusion for this tension occurs early as the child, through the development of reflective thought, can recognize the growing discrepancy between earlier experiences organized by wish expressed through fantasy and pretend, and later experiences organized by socialized thought, language, and the linear demands of cause and effect. Reflective thought also contributes to the child's awareness of the incongruity between his or her interpretation of an event and the interpretation of the same event by others. Those two dominant systems for organizing were described in detail by Piaget. The first ways of knowing are organized by preoperational thought (Piaget, 1962), the later experiences by concrete operational thought in middle childhood and operational thought in adolescence and adulthood (Piaget, 1954). There are parallels between these systems and Freud's primary and secondary process thought (Noy, 1973). The later-developing systems are characterized by the child's growing capacity to employ cognitively consistent concepts to recognize and to accommodate in less egocentric ways to the demands of external events. This limits the possibilities of fantasy as the process creates awareness of the need to adapt to an expanding world that extends beyond the immediate world of the child. The first ways of knowing are being merged with socialized-logical thought, with the awareness of a vast world beyond immediate control that is a threat to self similar to the awareness that the mother is not always available to provide pleasure and reduce anxiety. The transitional object served to reduce this conflict of awareness. For the older child with more social awareness, the need for control is met by the use of a special fantasy that incorporates egocentric wish with cosmic social order and predictability.

CREATING A KNOWABLE WORLD: PARACOSMS

Found sometimes in younger children but more often in children between ages eight and thirteen, paracosmic fantasy (Cohen & MacKeith, 1991) develops during the time children demonstrate a growing capacity to use language and think in more socialized ways (Piaget, 1954) and a more articulate capacity for reflective thought (Noy, 1979). These private worlds are always well organized, with the fantasy being maintained and elaborated upon over an extended period of time. Often private, but sometimes shared, the fantasy has emotional meaning to the child similar to that of the transitional object. The paracosmic creation is important to the child and is rewarding. The child looks forward to the time of day when paracosm play and story can take place. It is important to the child that this created world be internally consistent. The content of the story unfolding in the paracosm may be related to a story the child is familiar with, and the structure of the place may be related to a place the child really knows. Favorite toys and dolls often play roles in the stories. However, the range of fantasy is broad, and includes imaginary islands and countries with people who live only in the child's imagination. Private language and means of communication known only to the child are used in these special places and guarantee the child's ownership. However, although the world is idyllic and private, the paracosm always contains important elements that correspond to real experience.

A paracosm usually comes to an end by the late teens. However, during their existence they can maintain the emotional involvement of the child for five or more years, and are often remembered fondly long into adulthood. Although not every child who has had a paracosm is later found to be exceptionally creative, it is interesting to note that many eminently creative authors have had such fantasies as children. The list includes, but is not limited to, Thomas de Quincey, Anthony Trollope, Friedrich Nietzsche, Robert Louis Stevenson, C. S. Lewis, and the four authors discussed in this book. The wish to control and understand experience through the dominance of wish is basic to the creation of the paracosm. It is a private world representing conclusions based on first ways of knowing and conclusions that require an interpretation based on alternative systems involving socialized thought. The paracosm as a conclusion to the tension between the two ways of knowing is a creative act in childhood, and the psychological need behind this creative act may continue into adulthood. Emily Brontë engaged in paracosmic fantasies as a child and as a young woman. J. M. Barrie shared his first paracosm with his mother. At age eight, Jack Kerouac developed an elaborate world of an imaginary racetrack in which he reduced the chance of winning or losing by handicapping his imaginary horses. Isak Dinesen's identification as a male was expressed in the paracosm she created with her sisters.

MEMORY AND THE EMPTY PAGE

When Emily Brontë, J. M. Barrie, Isak Dinesen, and Jack Kerouac sat before the empty page and began their stories, they did so because they needed to construct a memory to understand loss. All of them were able to create the intensity of the immediate experience felt by Tyrone as an eight-year-old in the stress of transition and redefinition of self, and all were unique in that their memory of the experience of loss was organized by the first ways of knowing. Their art was to take these early images and tell their stories in the emotional metaphors that attract us to their works. Because their memories were acquired at a time when the difference between "me" and "not me" was not well established, the psychological merger with the lost individual continued in important ways in the memory and lives of all four writers. Their stories are enriched by the capacity to animate experiences found in childhood thought, and their major literary characters live in a romantic paracosmic fantasy of loss. With childhood egocentrism, Heathcliff is insulted by the power of death to remove a lover who is a part of his self, and Peter Pan thinks death could be a great adventure. In Isak Dinesen's story "Roads Around Pisa," Pellegrina, faced with the narcissistic insult of the loss of her creative self, her beautiful voice, leaps like a ghostly bird off a mountain. Obsessed with the death of his older brother, Jack Kerouac says about himself, "I am made of loss."

Most people maintain some of the richness of the first ways of knowing as they organize their everyday experience in the sometimes prosaic reciprocity required in the world of the adult. Access to these memories enriches all experience, but the capacity for social exchange and reciprocity with others requires significant shifts away from the egocentrism and narcissism of the child. Although the four authors were enriched by their childhood memories, they were also prisoners of their preoccupations with the conflicts generated at that time. It was the inability to reach a conclusion about the early loss of love and the capacity to obtain love that was a source of their creativity but a detriment to their capacity to understand themselves and use reciprocity in understanding others. In their lives they were bound to understand the important things through their first understanding and enduring memories of loss.

CHAPTER 2

Imagination and the Shock of Recognition

> Intelligence thus begins neither with knowledge of self nor of things as such but with knowledge of their interaction, and by orienting itself simultaneously toward the two poles of that interaction intelligence organizes the world by organizing itself.
>
> Jean Piaget, *The Construction of Reality in the Child* (1954)

THE FAMILY ROMANCE

The psychological make-up of the child such as his or her level and balance of egocentric and reflective thought and ability to modulate affect to understand experience, contributes to the determination of how events will be interpreted. However, it is the interpersonal experiences of love and trust that will greatly determine imagination and how memory over time will finally define events in the past. The evolving dimensions of self can be explored in pretend play, but it is within the context of the family that the child is forced into an awareness and a definition of self, in the framework of having love or losing love. Transitional objects and paracosms demonstrate both the power of imagination and its limitations. The full range of the child's need for love and trust cannot be met by pretend play. The full range and richness of love and trust can only be developed by the child's accommodating to the growing awareness that as a person, he or she exists in the context of other persons, who, unlike transitional objects, come and go independent of wish. Over time the child acquires the knowledge that needs and desires can be met by acquiring the capacity for reciprocity: modulating one's wishes with an awareness of the wishes of the person one desires.

This process of reciprocity clearly involves some awareness of one's own inner states, an awareness of the inner states of those one loves, and, most importantly, the interaction required to sustain the relationship (Noam, 1988).

This major interpersonal-emotional development is confounded with the awareness that even with less egocentric attempts at love, the source of love may be inconsistent and others may compete for the love available. A new emotional state of jealousy, with the corresponding affects of frustration and anger, is generated and seeks articulation and representation in reflective thought. In the classic Oedipal conflict, developing socialized thought will provide the four- to six-year-old boy with the relative comparison of bigger than or less than, yet egocentrism will cause him to confuse his own competitive wishes with those of the rival. This egocentric confusion exists regardless of the sex of the child, or whether it is the father or other sibs who are the competitors, or whether the source of love is one parent or the other or any sib. The emerging representations involved are multiple and greatly dependent on the child's perception of the rival and the loved person. Importantly, the content of reflective thought involves emerging and poorly articulated aggressive and sexual components that are part of an evolving representation of self and others that had not previously been the subject of awareness and ownership. These emerging representations become sources of anxiety as their possible future implications are explored and vaguely understood in fantasy.

Although reflective thought develops between ages two and eight, it is between the ages of four and eight that the first ways of knowing and the developing new ways of understanding experiences are being integrated into an awareness of self. The representative images of love, aggression, and frustration and the full range of human emotions become part of the child's understanding of those people who make up his or her emotional life. The capacity to remember past events is enhanced now by a more detailed awareness of immediate events and a growing awareness of the future. It is the profound impact of the awareness in fantasy of the possibility of having love and losing it over time that greatly determines the development of reflective thought or, in other terms, thoughts about self and others that are subject to conscious manipulation and exploration. These fantasies evolve over time into a self that seeks love in the context of aggressive and sexual wishes that have to be consciously accepted as part of that self. The child's first images of love and competition for this love involve evaluations of self that are influenced by the evaluations of those he or she loves. This developing social awareness generates negative connotations of self that are also sources of anxiety. The source of the anxiety is a function of the egocentric perception of internal and external events. The central issue is ownership of the conflicted wish. If the anxiety is reduced by fantasies replacing these wishes rather than by ongoing experience in relationships, an understanding that could develop through conscious reflective thought is now beyond that system. Poorly understood, powerful, enduring memories begin to be constructed. Because of anxiety, these thoughts cannot be expressed and explored consciously in the full emotional range of relationships. Memories of these first loves find expression in ways that reduce anxiety and guilt through enduring fantasies protective of self. At the same time, these fantasies limit the capacity to understand and experience love through reciprocity. The psychological awareness of me–not me is now confounded by a new cognitive organization that serves to reduce threatening affect by constricting reflective thought: the unconscious (Noy, 1979).

During childhood and throughout life, anxiety can be reduced by compensatory fantasies. In terms of the growth of the ability to love, for most people the use of fantasy to reduce anxiety is not pervasive but temporary, as the opportunities to explore and understand love and establish trust with the full range of affect and intelligence remain available. As these opportunities are available, the understanding of love expands beyond the narcissism and limitations of childhood thought. This new love is enriched by the individual's confidence in the capacity to obtain love and an articulate awareness of self and others as the basis of relationships. In this situation, awareness of self is autonomous, expands with experience throughout life, and is enriched by the original fantasies of childhood and first ways of knowing that are not frozen in time by anxiety.

It is important to note that although childhood fantasies may reduce intolerable levels of affect such as anxiety and guilt, they never completely mitigate such affects. Only interpersonal experience that simultaneously reduces the affect and increases the awareness of self and others is sufficient. By decreasing the individual's unconscious motivations, thereby separating memory from fantasies of the past, reflective thought can expand awareness and mitigate intolerable levels of affect. In most cases the fantasies generated at the time of early loss may reduce anxiety but do not completely erase the fearful memories of the death of the family member and the morbid conclusions, motivated by guilt, that contribute to chronic states of anxiety and depression.

EARLY LOSS AND MOURNING

Creative children are frequently found in families where intellectual exploration, unique perspective, and original ideas are encouraged by the parents (Singer & Singer, 1990), and creative adults frequently come from families that were characterized by relative emotional harmony and support for family members. However, there is considerable evidence that many creative individuals come from families that were not supportive or even accepting of creative efforts, and severe family conflicts and general disharmony were common (Albert, 1978). The contribution of the family experience to an individual's creative abilities is really unknown and is probably multiple. Each family is different, and even a harmonious family can become less well organized and supportive of the child under commonly occurring stressors such as the serious illness of a family member, financial failures, divorce, and death.

The child's initial understanding of death is that it is a transitory state such as sleep. Understood in this way, it is like something experienced and therefore knowable; loved ones, including pets, can return. Eventually, the child knows that death is a permanent state beyond experience and that no one returns. This knowledge is the beginning of the child's awareness of his or her vulnerability and existential link with all of nature (Vanderberg, 1991). The immediate effect of the child's experience of the death of a family member is an individual matter and depends on factors such as who has died, the culture and religion of the family, and the circumstances of the death (Cain, Fast, & Erickson, 1964). Children react differently to the death of a parent (Pollack, 1962) and the death of a sibling (Pollack, 1978). The latter often generates ambivalent feelings of loss as well as some satisfaction in the removal of a rival for parental affection. As was true of Jack Kerouac's experience, a prolonged serious illness of a sibling may require that parents devote time caring for the sick child. Because of the possibility of death, the sick child's value to the parents increases, and more open demonstrations of love are displayed. Meanwhile, the child who is well may get less attention and is responded to in the routine manner of everyday life. After the death, the parents' view of the remaining children shifts, as fulfillment of emotional needs and future goals and anticipations of success that were focused on the dead child may be transferred to the living.

For the remaining children this early adaptation to change and loss of either parent or sibling may be the first experience of the mourning process. The key issue is the incongruity between what the child feels about the loss and the view of significant family members. A successfully completed mourning involves coming to terms with the loss psychologically, both internally and interpersonally, with an exploration of the complex dimensions of affect involved. This can be a long-term process with the goal of freeing oneself from a person and event that exists only in memory. A positive outcome of the mourning process is a reduction of anxiety and sadness so that the memory of the event can be recalled and understood without intrusive, obligatory thought such as guilt. The process of understanding death and loss frequently takes a considerable amount of time for the child, and it can be made easier by having a sympathetic adult available who can tolerate the expression of the child's ambivalent feelings about the loss.

Brothers and sisters are often the objects of open expression of intense feelings of both affection and hostility that cannot be expressed toward a parent. In our case story (Chapter 4), Tyrone knew Lucas from his own experience with him, but his understanding of this rival whom he both loved and disliked was greatly influenced by his mother's demonstrated love and need for Lucas. Although sibs may be seen as competitors, they are also models for learning, identification, and definition of self. The child knows and evaluates the sib based on his or her own experience with that sib, but also through the evaluation expressed directly and indirectly by a parent. This was true of Jack Kerouac's experience of his older brother, Gerard, and the discrepancy between his parents' experience, especially his mother's, and his own experience was a chronic source of conflict. Kerouac's mother idealized Gerard before and after his death and was unable throughout Kerouac's life to let him forget his "sainted" dead brother. J. M. Barrie hardly knew his older brother, David, and his knowledge of him and identification with him were based on his mother's memories of David expressed during her own grieving process. Idealization of the dead that cannot be corrected by experience is critical in making the mourning process pathogenic (Pollack, 1978). J. M. Barrie's and Jack Kerouac's loss of an older sibling also illustrates the importance of birth order when the older sib, for particular reasons such as a serious illness or a tragic accident, acquires an authority that rivals the parents'.

The loss of a parent has similar psychological effects to the loss of a sib. However, the parent can be remembered as a powerful figure who was protective of the child and sympathetic to his or her wishes. Unlike a sibling, the parent can be remembered as a mythical figure who was distinct from other adults because of his or her great accomplishments. Isak Dinesen remembered her father as such a figure. The suicide of such a person, as in Dinesen's experience, always leaves the unanswerable question as to why such a horrible event occurred to such a powerful protector.

Emily Brontë is unique among all the individuals considered here. Only three years old when she lost her mother, she was raised by her two older sisters. Young girls themselves, they were both sisters and mothers to Emily. At a period of development when children are beginning to explore and understand trust in relationships, Brontë was being raised by children who were themselves in the process of grieving over the loss of their mother. When Brontë was seven, both of her caregiving sisters died in the same year. At a time when her basic sense of self was being established, Brontë experienced loss as a disruption to her sense of trust and sense of self. Living in the confines of their small home, Brontë must have witnessed or been in close proximity to the event of the death of her three caregivers. The reaction of Brontë as a child to such a series of tragic losses is found in her novel *Wuthering Heights*. After the death of Cathy, those who live at Wuthering Heights are orphans, and the mad man who dominates their lives is himself an orphan, obsessed with death and in search of a part of himself that was lost when Cathy died.

Before the entry of death and early loss, Tyrone, Emily Brontë, J. M. Barrie, Isak Dinesen, and Jack Kerouac had known love and trust in a more stable atmosphere. Relationships were ordered in particular patterns of predictability. Death changed all that, abruptly and irreversibly. Because of the stress in the family, unsuccessful grieving occurs when the child cannot comfortably explore and accept what the death and loss of the family member means to him or her both interpersonally and internally. The consequence is a formation of a false sense of self and a limitation of the child's capacity to imagine that can endure into adulthood. The effect on imagination has an effect on the memory of death and loss.

LOSS AND MEMORY

It is in the nature of childhood thought and emotion that these individuals the child loves are also competitors for love and targets of jealousy and anger. Like adults, children are ambivalent. It takes time and experience to sort out and understand ambivalence and love. This sorting out requires a capacity to reflect on self and one's experience. If the child experiences the death of an important family member, such as a sibling or a parent, then, because of the stress in the family, both sides of the ambivalent feeling can no longer be expressed and explored in the family but can only be known by fantasy. The fantasies and emotions of childhood are intense, and when associated with anxiety they cannot be consciously explored and sorted out as part of love. As the child develops, anxiety-laden memories of loss take on particular characteristics that are unlike anxiety-free memories of experience. Because these memories are less accessible to reflective thought, they do not go through the usual developmental transformation and synthesis but remain represented by images acquired during a less differentiated period of cognitive development. Because of anxiety, reflective thought does not function adequately with these isolated memories and, consequently, autonomous thought is not acquired for these events (Noy, 1979). Another characteristic of these images is that they become obligatory and intrusive, and the individual is compelled to explore them repeatedly through actions and preoccupation with inadequate reduction of the anxiety and unsatisfactory resolution of the conflicts.

Because the individual's sense of historical self is known through events organized by first ways of knowing that cannot be reflected upon, explored, and modified, a part of the self is functionally psychologically divided (Noam, 1988). The sense of an autonomous self does not develop, and as an adult the individual may seek to regain or establish self-confidence and a new understanding of self through association and identification with other individuals perceived as having the needed characteristics that he or she does not have. The individual often attempts to establish a sense of trust in these relationships that was not available from important individuals who, though physically present at the initial experience, were not available emotionally for the child. Interpersonal events that can generate anxiety and disrupt the development of self are multiple, but the death of a sibling or parent is a high-risk event for this process. When loss is followed by experience that does not allow it to be adequately examined by reflective thought and incorporated into consciousness as part of the grieving process, the loss will continue to be known essentially as the child originally understood it. In this situation, affect-laden memory intrudes on new experience as the maturing individual attempts to understand his or her past and create a different definition of self. The dominant memory of the past is the memory of the lost love, and new relationships are often attempts to reconstruct the self through an experience that will provide a different and more desirable sense of self. In the process, the new love is understood in terms of romantic ideation, and the object of love is an extension of self.

THE WISH FOR PERFECTION

The original conflicted thoughts about death and loss of love can be replaced or transformed by a broad range of anxiety-reducing fantasies that limit the functions of imagination and reflective thought such as guilt, externalization, obsessive/compulsive ritual, and reaction formation. However, the defense that seems most pertinent to creative thought is identification. Resolution of the conflict of death and loss by fantasy results in an inarticulate image of self and intense feelings about trust that are associated with love, a sense of mystery, and the unexpected. It was the beginning awareness of a part of the self as imperfect and undesirable, generated during the loss of first love, that motivated the search for a figure that is self-sufficient, all powerful, and highly desirable: all the attributes the individual feels that he or she does not possess. Like the transitional object, models for identification are animated by imagination, acquiring qualities that reflect the wishes of the individual. At the time of loss, the child may cope with negative feelings about self by identifying with any available figure who can serve as a model. Often the child identifies with the lost sib or parent, who through death becomes the object of compensatory fantasies rather than experience. When memory of the lost love is based on the emotions of death and an unsatisfactory grieving process, first ways of knowing persist and a sense of imperfection determines the experience of new love.

Because of their histories and the power of the unconscious, such individuals seek new relationships that can serve to reduce the sense of imperfection while nurturing the wish for perfection. The new object of love is created to fulfill a troubled inner state. As with a fetish or idol, possessing or becoming like this idealized model becomes an intermediate step to being close to God in a religious sense or perfection in a psychological sense. However, because this motivation is based on conflict and wish, the model does not serve as a bridge to understand experience through reciprocity and differentiation of self but serves as a limited tutor to reconstruct a past memory and temporarily fulfill a wish. The romantic relationship is constructed by the unconscious and motivated by a compensatory wish to possess the essence of perfection. This psychological process, similar to the child's fantasy of the transitional object and imaginary companion, is supported in the adult by romantic ideation used to understand the experience with the idealized figure. It is a characteristic of romantic ideation to make the loved and idealized person an extension of self rather than an object of intimate experiences that expand the discrimination between self and other (Morrison & Morrison, 1988). All this is driven by the affective intensity of the memories of death and loss and the intense feeling of being alive and complete in the presence of the loved one. During the initial excitement of idealized romantic love, the lovers create a shared paracosm. Romantic ideation generates the idealized image of the lost love and the compensatory fantasy that death itself can be an idealized solution to the individual's profound sense of imperfection.

The fantasy of the sense of completeness in a perfect state is made fragile by attempts to generate it by experience. The nostalgia for loss and death may be maintained by embracing the dark answer of death as a conclusion to the chronic tension of trying to maintain such a childhood fantasy.

Constructed by childhood memory, where death is never experienced in the more articulate and socially elaborate awareness of adolescence and adulthood, the lost sibling or parent can be created by need and wish and can therefore be perfect. This may be enhanced by the remaining family members, who most often harmonize the memories of the lost one based on idealization, or at times more negative conclusions, rather than memories reflecting that person in the context of experience. Thus the "truth" of the experience is highlighted by conflicted ideas not explored and images protected by romantic ideation, lack of experience, defensive identification, and the collective memories of the remaining family members. This psychological truth of the memory of death can be the basis for the conclusion that death itself is a transforming process rather than an end state. Because this memory is constructed by the intense fantasies of the unconscious, it is alive in ways that are different from memories less burdened with anxiety. For example, the surviving individual may over time develop nostalgia for death. In a counter-phobic reaction, the individual constructs supportive myths and legends that nurture the need to avoid the original experience of loss. The power of death itself lives to construct a memory of it that reflects the egocentrism and fantasy characteristic of the first ways of knowing and the wish of the child to have a different conclusion regarding that power. When death is chosen as a conclusion to conflicts of idealized love, one or both lovers believe that death is a transition to a state of reunion and perfection, rather than a conclusion of the frustrated search. The lovers seek a final and enduring paracosm.

These intense memories organized by the first ways of knowing were vital roots for creativity for the writers of loss who are the focus of this book. Their memories motivated them to search for perfection. Fueled by romantic ideation, they found idealized objects of love who were muses as well. The psychological links between the romantic ideation used to create the idealized figure of love and the function of the muse as the idealized figure are numerous.

ROMANTIC IDEATION AND THE MUSE

When the lover has a sense of imperfection, the possessing of the idealized lover, and being worthy of that love, helps the lover create a sense of self as complete and perfect. This fantasy of imperfection develops after the loss of first love, and the motivation for new love is to explore a vaguely understood part of self through possession of the idealized person in an idealized world. The psychological need for the transitional object and paracosmic states are combined. In this wished-for world, the beloved will reciprocate in feeling, ideas, and sexuality, not in terms of common prosaic experience and everyday thought but rather in the systems of the first ways of knowing in which narcissistic love was beginning to be explored and then, because of anxiety, was organized by the fantasies of the unconscious. It is the unconscious with its intruding influence on the development of the awareness of self that generates the motivation to master the past through the will to create. For the creative individual who wishes to tell a story with a different conclusion to the original story of loss, the new lover is a source of identification as well as inspiration. This inspiration is most often found in the lover whose own unconscious motivation finds a match in the relationship and then responds and interacts in the richness of shared romantic ideation. The interaction of the idealized lovers is an inspiration to create that is an external and internal matrix of creative narratives and conclusions for both. Because of the fusion of self and other, the original source of inspiration is sometimes lost. The key to this is the original excitement of first discovery when both lovers sense the commonality of views and interpretation of experience. The source of inspiration may be in a shared experience that results in being remembered as an ideal state: for example, the shared hunting expeditions of Isak Dinesen and Denys Finch-Hatton, or the intense on-the-road experience shared by Jack Kerouac and Neal Cassady. It is significant that these experiences are retold as romanticized adventures that are associated with death. In the telling of these shared adventures, the idealized figure and event are presented in romantic and at times mythic portrayals. The powerful role of projection in this process is seen in J. M. Barrie's search for the lost and idealized David and his capacity to enlist the replicas of David as his androgynous muse of creation (Morrison & Morrison, 1988).

The psychological capacity to seek and at the same time construct the muse of creation is seen in Emily Brontë's poem *The Visitant.* This voice of inspiration in her poetry is experienced by Brontë as external and not entirely comforting. She seems to have concretized and externalized her own internal state and is acknowledging to herself that her creativity is not always under her conscious control. She does this again in the psychological merger of Heathcliff and Cathy, when both admit that sense of self is centered in the other. Considering Brontë's history of early loss, it is significant that even after Cathy's death, Heathcliff is still possessed by her. Her absence over time does not fade in memory but becomes the basis of a more intense morbid preoccupation. This "love" becomes destructive to Heathcliff and all the "children" who are under his control.

The writer feels that he or she needs the muse to create and sometimes only feels creative in the actual presence of this figure. The source of inspiration may be in the lifestyle of the muse, an attitude, its perceived beauty, or the ability to transform ordinary experience into a more fantastic state. The muse is often seen as having a significant attribute related to creativity that the writer does not feel he or she possesses. This attribute is often seen as crucial for creativity and can be possessed only by being in the presence of the muse and possessing its affection and trust.

THE MASTERY OF DEATH

Successful grieving and mourning allow the child to come to terms with one of the great mysteries of life, which is death. Under these conditions, to the degree possible, the child will acquire some psychological mastery of death. Unsuccessful grieving and mourning restrict imagination, understanding, and mastery. As will be seen with Tyrone (Chapter 4), the child who has just experienced death and early loss is quite different from the adult who has had the experience as a child. The major difference is that the adult who has experienced unsuccessful mourning has had time to create a memory of the event that supports a fragile sense of self and a limited mastery. Both the child and the adult will demonstrate preoccupations that influence the use of imagination and compulsions to explore and express their confused understanding of this event. The child can use all the modalities for imaginative expression such as drawing, dancing, and pretend play. In any case, this use of imagination will not result in psychological mastery without a supportive adult, such as a relative or a therapist, who helps the child explore the full range of internal and interpersonal meaning of death and early loss. The child will have to recognize, understand, and own his or her motivation. Adults with a history of early loss and unsuccessful grieving lack psychological mastery of death and demonstrate enduring limitations of their imagination. The confused exploration and search for understanding will find expression in relationships and repetitious efforts to retell the story. Like therapy, repetition of thought and emotion without a focus on the conflicted meaning of the memory for the individual will not result in growth and change. Retelling the story has a cathartic effect, but only in a trusting interpersonal context that encourages reflective thought can change occur.

For the writer affected by loss, the first encounter as a child was with death and then the loss of love. This encounter generated the fearful and poorly understood experience that motivates the writer to make it more understandable, in a story that is more acceptable to self. It is an attempt at mastery. In this process of reducing the tensions of the past by inventing a new self, the writer creates. The first encounter with death and loss influences imagination, but also action. Obsessed by loss, the adult individual seeks intense relationships and experiences that psychologically parallel the first experience of love and loss, with the important difference that the adult feels more in control. However, unlike the retelling of the story in imagination, the redoing of the story for the writers examined in this text was not under their control. For each one, death and the transitory nature of romantic love dominated their adult lives, as was true when they were children. In their relationships they tried to deny the finality of death with lovers who seemed protected from that finality.

Confronted with the mystery of death and the shock of recognition of his own motivations, Tyrone, as a child, creates a magical basketball player in an idealized basketball game that will allow him for a time to distance himself from death and self-awareness. The creation of this imaginary game in which he is the passive opponent of a powerful adversary is a wish to continue an idealized past, construct a wished-for future, and maintain a love that was lost. The four authors of loss considered here constructed an idealized memory of lost love, and they tried to maintain love through a romantic ideation that was beyond the prosaic limitation of compassionate love. In their lives they were never able to sustain their wished-for paracosmic existence, as death continued its implacable claim on their experience. However, turning to their art and their creations—Heathcliff, Peter Pan, Pellegrina Leoni, and Dean Moriarty—they created stories that denied the dominance of death and transformed their experience of love into art.

CHAPTER 3

Memories of Loss

You go and don't come back.
Benny, age 6

Generally, children do not think much about death. There are many events closer to their experiences that will be of interest to them. It is usually the death of a pet that gets their attention. The child's understanding of such an event depends on age, cognitive capacity, family structures, and experience (Stambrook & Parker, 1987). Like everything the child knows, the understanding will also be a function of an evolving awareness of the permanence of objects and an evolving sense of self, merged with imagination. A three-year-old may see death as sleep or an illness. It is not permanent, and the animal or person might wake up or take some medicine and then be all right. From ages three to eight, children demonstrate an increasing awareness that even if an object disappears or changes in appearance, it continues to exist (Piaget, 1954). However, it is clear that something different has occurred when an animal or person dies, and the object that is dead may be experiencing events in a different way. For example, it could be just like things usually are but under changed circumstances. Perhaps a dead person can sense what is going on but cannot move. The dead person may be lonely and scared. The affective tone of the child will also reflect the personal relevance of the loss and how the child's family responds to the event.

The family's religion and the family relationships can have a significant effect. Having older members of the family such as grandparents may result in the child concluding that death is associated with old age and is final but remote. It only happens to older people, who are really different from the peers that the child knows. Such a conclusion, combined with the family's view that there is an afterlife, is comforting even when the grandfather or grandmother really does disappear. The actual experience of death appears to accelerate the child's understanding that death is an end state and that the dead are in a different, insensitive condition from the living. With the growing capacity to use stable cognitive constructs to understand experiences and the related capacity for reflective thought, the child between the ages of six and eight comes to the conclusion that everyone will die, including himself (Cohen et al., 2002). Although this conclusion is found to be somewhat consistent in this age range, the idea of the source of death as being internal or external varies. Fantasies of a "death man" coming to claim the victim or even the "bad driver" are examples of ideas about external causes of death held by children. This changes after age nine as children see death as due to an internal cause, even if related to an accident, and as final and universal.

There have been efforts to conceptualize the child's understanding of death by both Freudian theorists (Yalom, 1980) and Piagetian theorists (Kastenbaum & Aisenberg, 1972). In orthodox psychoanalytic theory, the child would have no concerns about death until after the Oedipal period, and then only if the conflicts of that complex were unresolved. Theorists using Piaget's developmental model conclude that the pre-adolescent child cannot understand death as irreversible, because of the limitations of concrete cognitive thinking dominant during this period. During adolescence, the capacity to use formal operations to form abstract concepts enables the individual to understand the event of death. The point is that children in the preoperational stage cannot understand death as irreversible, whereas a child in the operational stage, capable of conservation, can use this logical capacity to grasp this definition of death.

The application of either Freudian or Piagetian theory may be useful in the conceptualization of the child's understanding of death, but both theories have significant limitations. Research support for many of the key Freudian theoretical concepts, such as the Oedipal complex, as originally presented, is not strong (Baldwin, 1967). Although a developmental sequence in cognitive awareness such as presented in Piaget's theory is useful, the failure to consider the interpersonal emotional factors that contribute to cognitive development limits that usefulness (Fast, 1985). After age two or so, the child's individual experience may generally have more influence on his or her understanding of death than does the particular psychosexual or cognitive stage the child is in. This is illustrated in the story of Benny, Robo-Man, and Dusty.

BENNY IN THE MIDDLE

Benny was five years old and having a difficult time in his pre-school. The pre-school was a socially prestigious place with a strong pre-academic curriculum. It was thought that the children who graduated from the program would have the intellectual skills that would place them in the upper 5 to 10% of their first-grade class. There was a major focus on learning how to read, and Benny was having a difficult time. He was also beginning to have a behavior problem. In the class he was seen by the teachers as aggressive and a "clown." His attention and concentration were poor. On the playground, he seemed very insecure and needy for attention. He was large for his age and was starting to have angry outbursts with the other children. The teachers thought he had a learning disability and attention deficit disorder.

There were indications that Benny might not make it much longer in the pre-school. He was referred to a psychologist in private practice who was an expert in learning disabilities as well as a therapist. Both of Benny's parents were physicians. Steven, the father, was an anesthesiologist at the county hospital. He came from a very wealthy family and, based on his inheritance, he didn't have to work. In his early forties, he was a large, handsome man who saw himself as a professional but was most clearly invested in sailing his racing-class sailboat. He sailed every chance he had and would take a month-long vacation, sailing with a crew that were his close friends. Sandra, Benny's mother, was also in her early forties. She was the director of a childhood asthma clinic in the Department of Pediatrics at the University Medical School. She was an associate professor and was recognized nationally for her research on childhood asthma. Although attractive, she spent little time on her appearance or dress. Benny was to be her only child. It was through Sandra and her professional connections that Benny was brought to see Dr. Gill, the psychologist, who was also on the faculty of the Medical School.

Dr. Gill arranged a meeting with the parents before he scheduled his meeting with Benny. It took considerable effort to arrange the meeting because of everyone's busy schedules. When the time came for the meeting, Steven failed to appear. He called Dr. Gill's office an hour before to say that he had an emergency at the hospital. Sandra frowned when she was told that Steven was not coming but said nothing about it. Benny's birth and developmental history were unremarkable. He was a wanted baby. Sandra said that he was no problem at home. He had had the same woman, Maria, as his caregiver since he was two years old. Maria picked him up from school. Steven and Sandra took turns taking him to school. As the interview continued, it was clear that Benny's time with his parents was often a function of their crowded professional schedules. Sandra said that his father wanted to have more time with Benny on the sailboat, but she felt the boy was too young for that.

Benny looked a good deal like his father. During the evaluation with Dr. Gill, his attention and concentration were adequate. He was comfortable with Dr. Gill. Midway through the testing, he turned to Dr. Gill and asked him if he was a doctor. Dr. Gill said that he was. Benny then asked him if he had a first name. When Dr. Gill said his first name was Karl, Benny said that he was going to call him Karl. Dr. Gill laughed, said that was fine, and asked why. Benny frowned and said he couldn't remember. Dr. Gill made a note and continued the evaluation. Benny became agitated and oppositional on test items that required him to organize sequenced auditory information and again on tasks that required him to integrate sequenced information presented both visually and auditorily. His scores on visual sequencing tasks were low-average. His scores on auditory sequencing tasks were a standard deviation below average, as was his score on the task requiring the integration of sequenced visual and auditory information. Benny's scores on the remaining subtest requiring the organization of simultaneous information was in the high-average to above-average range. The pattern of scores on the evaluation indicated the possibility that Benny might develop a learning disability that would interfere with his ability to learn to read (Kaufman & Kaufman, 1983).

Dr. Gill had scheduled another meeting with the parents to discuss the evaluation. Again Steven did not attend. When Dr. Gill discussed his absence with Sandra, she suggested that he call her husband to arrange the next appointment. She was very upset about the test results. Dr. Gill asked permission to talk to Benny's teacher. Sandra was reluctant. Only after Dr. Gill said that he would not discuss the results with the teacher but wanted to gather more information did Sandra agree. When Dr. Gill met with Benny's teacher she presented the results of the school's pre-academic tests, which confirmed his results. The teacher said she thought that Benny was not appropriate for the program and was thinking about discussing this with the parents. She also said that Benny's relationships at school were getting worse. She hesitated a moment, then added that she was concerned about his play. She said that about two months ago he brought a toy Robo-Man to school. At first the teachers agreed to let him keep it in his locker, but he began taking it to the schoolyard. Benny would play by himself as Robo-Man and terminated a number of unseen robots from space. Benny was angry when he was not allowed to bring Robo-Man to school any more. He was now pretending to be Robo-Man. The teacher told Dr. Gill that this had happened this week. She also said that she had informed Benny's parents of her concerns about his play.

Before Dr. Gill was able to contact Benny's parents about the school conference, he had a call from an upset Sandra. In a fight over a ball, Benny had hit a girl in the face and pulled her hair. When a teacher attempted to stop Benny, he hit her. Dr. Gill met with the parents immediately after their conference with the teachers. They were informed that Benny could not continue at the school as a student. Steven attended the school meeting and the meeting with Dr. Gill. Initially the session with Dr. Gill was about the school. Both parents felt they had not been appropriately informed about Benny's problems and they were angry. Sandra was surprised when Steven said that one morning as he dropped Benny off he had had a conversation with the teacher and that she had told him of her concerns about Benny. Sandra was angry and said this was a typical example of Steven never telling her anything. He responded that it was difficult to communicate with her because she was never around. At this point each parent accused the other of being the source of Benny's problem. Dr. Gill found himself in the middle of two angry people who really hadn't shared their feelings for some time. At the end of the hour Sandra asked Dr. Gill to see Benny in therapy. Dr. Gill said he thought it was needed but that he would have to see both parents to evaluate the family situation further.

BENNY AND ROBO-MAN

Maria brought Benny for his appointment. When he entered the playroom, he brought a box of Robo-Man transformer toys of assorted sizes and destructive capacities. He spent time demonstrating how each could be made into various objects such as tanks and guns and then be reconstructed into powerful Robo-Man figures. This took almost all the session. In the end he gave Dr. Gill one of the smaller robots and took the rest. He told Dr. Gill to build a fort because his army was going to attack. The play had hardly begun when Dr. Gill said it was time to end. He asked Benny if he had any problems he wanted to talk about. He said no. As Benny loaded his toys, Dr. Gill said that he was going to meet with him and his parents to see if they could make things go better for him at school and at home. As Benny left he said that his mom had said the same thing. He added that he didn't like school.

Maria always brought Benny for his appointment. The theme of the play was consistent. Benny directed it and allowed Dr. Gill little room to insert any variation. Benny built himself an elaborate fort out of blocks. He gave Dr. Gill's robot the name of R2-D2, or R2. After Benny's robots had used most of the blocks, R2 could build his fort. R2 was completely in the dark as to what the war was about and defended himself against the attack of Benny's army by hiding under a block and hoping he would not get hurt. Taking the role of R2, Dr. Gill portrayed him as being alone against powerful aggressive forces. R2 didn't know what the war was about or where the enemy came from, but he wanted help. Benny gave R2 a female doll from the ones available in the playroom. He named her Princess Lila. Dr. Gill gave her an active role in the battles, but she was ineffective against the robots.

During one of the first interviews with the parents, Steven made it clear that the only problem Benny had was that his mother didn't know how to set limits for him when she was at home. He said that Maria was Benny's mother. At first, Sandra reacted with anger and said that all Steven knew was how to avoid relating to Benny except to give him things. Steven had given Benny the Robo-Man toys. The meetings with Dr. Gill were characterized by the couple's angry outbursts and accusations. It was difficult to get them to focus on Benny. Sandra became more defensive regarding Steven's comments about her being an inadequate and part-time mother. After four meetings Dr. Gill said he would meet with them monthly to support his work with Benny, but they must enter couples' therapy. He gave them the names of several therapists.

Benny came once a week and always brought his robots. The robots were consistently aggressive, but a major theme was how they could change. R2 and Princess Lila would recognize them as they attacked and left their fort. Each

Robo-Man had a name and would stay for a while and then leave. As each robot left the fort, Benny would rearrange its parts. One in particular, with the name of Strange Man, would appear often with various changes. When the robots attacked again, Lila and R2 would yell, "Who are these guys? They keep changing!" Dr. Gill would say, "You never know who you can trust." Dr. Gill tried through his role as R2 to help Benny explore the source of the anger and lack of trust. After five sessions with these themes there was a shift. Benny brought the Robo-Man toys, but putting them aside he went to the large box of blocks. He built the robot fort in one corner of the room and then began to use the flat rectangular blocks as some sort of a road. This road took a great deal of time to build, and Benny made sure the blocks fitted together. He turned to Dr. Gill and asked him to help. Using almost all the blocks they extended the bridge from one corner of the room to the playhouse in the other corner. Benny next pulled out one of the large toy trucks and told Dr. Gill that they were movers. They took out the furniture from the playhouse, and when the house was empty Benny asked Dr. Gill to move the playhouse. At this point their time was almost over, and when Benny was told they would have to clean up the room he said "No." He wanted to leave it as it was. This resulted in a rage attack as Benny started to throw the blocks. He yelled at Dr. Gill that he had other kids that used the room and he, Benny, hated them. Dr. Gill managed to stop him before he threw the blocks at him, but he had to do most of the cleaning up.

Dr. Gill had only seen Sandra once in the two months since their last meeting. At that one appointment she had arrived 20 minutes late because of an emergency on the pediatric unit. Dr. Gill hadn't heard from Steven. He called Sandra and told her he had to talk to her immediately. When she returned the call, Dr. Gill told her he was not sure he could continue seeing Benny with his parents' limited participation. She came to the office the next day. She told Dr. Gill that Steven had moved out. He had had a girlfriend for some time, as Sandra had suspected. Steven had moved in with his new friend not long after their last meeting with Dr. Gill. He told Sandra that he wasn't interested in couples' therapy. There was nothing in their marriage worth saving. Sandra had an attractive face. During the time she was telling all of this she was more or less matter-of-fact. Occasionally her voice would become high pitched and her face would distort grotesquely as she would start to cry. She quickly suppressed the urge and went on in a normal way. She was in the middle of talking about the bickering with Steven when Dr. Gill broke in and asked how she thought Benny was experiencing this. She looked away and put her hand over her mouth as her eyes began to tear up. Dr. Gill said that she and Benny must be hurt and sad. One more grotesque face and an attempt to suppress it, and Sandra burst into uncontrollable crying.

It was some time before she was able to talk. Even then, her conversation was interspersed with tears. Sandra spoke mostly about herself, her anger, and how hurt and sad she was. Benny was being moved back and forth between his mother's and father's homes. The home of Steven's new friend, Megan, was in a nearby city across the bay. It was connected to where Sandra lived by a large suspension bridge. Sandra and Steven knew Megan socially before the split. Megan, who had been divorced for some time, had two boys of her own, one who was nine years old and another who was twelve. They lived with Megan. Although Benny wanted to be with his father, he was not getting along with Megan's boys. Steven had already hired a divorce attorney. Sandra wanted Dr. Gill to talk to Steven. He replied that he would think about talking to Steven if he called to say he was interested. Dr. Gill said he would continue with Benny only if Sandra would come in weekly to see him. She agreed to this arrangement.

When Benny returned for play therapy, Dr. Gill told him he knew that his mother and father were having troubles and that his time with Dr. Gill was important to him. He told Benny that they would work together to get through these bad times. The sequence in the following play therapy first consisted of building a solid road and bridge between two houses and moving all the families from one house to the next. This play was remarkable because the focus was on moving both families back and forth in the truck with little content regarding the families when they got to either home. In the next sequence, people fell out of the truck as they crossed the bridge. Sometimes because of a storm the bridge would break up and start floating away. Mothers, fathers, and children fell off the drifting parts of the bridge into the water and floated away. Neither parents nor children helped each other. As this play continued, Benny and Dr. Gill built a fortress-like home connected to the playhouse by the bridge. This new home had many doors. The play now consisted of the hazards of the trips back and forth to the houses as well as people going in and out of the rooms slamming doors. Dr. Gill used the themes of the play to support Benny in the difficulties of having two families where no one got along or supported each other.

DUSTY

Dr. Gill always picked up Benny in the waiting room after his secretary called to let him know that he had arrived. One day she called and said that Benny was there and that he had a surprise for him. When he arrived in the waiting room, Benny had a puppy in his lap. Both Maria and Benny had big smiles. The puppy was a golden Labrador retriever and his name was Dusty. Benny insisted on bringing Dusty to the playroom. While there he wanted Dr. Gill to hold Dusty. They played together with Dusty for the hour as Benny told Dr. Gill what a wonderful friend Dusty was. As he looked admiringly at his dog, Benny said that he had hair the same color as Dusty's. They ate and slept together. Except when Benny had to go to school they were always together. Dusty clearly enjoyed the relationship as he licked Benny's face and bounded around the playroom. Dr. Gill laughed and told Benny that he had a good buddy now that he could count on.

In his meetings with Sandra, Dr. Gill found out that she had bought Dusty for Benny. She felt that he was by himself too much when he was at her home.

When he visited Steven it was clear that he was by himself, or his father would take him out to shop sometimes. Megan's boys were very unhappy about sharing their home with their mother's new boyfriend and son. Steven tried to get the boys interested in sailing. They all went out on the boat one weekend and Benny was seasick the whole time. Steven hadn't told Sandra he was going to take Benny out on the boat and she was furious. She now had her own lawyer, and the divorce was becoming more hostile. At first Benny took Dusty with him when he visited his father. However, over time it was established that one of Megan's sons was allergic to dog hair. The allergy was severe, and the boy also developed a rash. It was agreed that Dusty had to stay home. This resulted in Benny refusing to go with his father. Steven became very angry, and there was a heated argument between Sandra and Steven that Benny witnessed. Eventually Benny agreed to visit his father, but when he was there he spent most of his time alone playing with his Robo-Man set. Sandra was concerned that Benny was becoming depressed. He had refused to go to his school. Sandra had found a private school that accepted children with learning and behavior problems. Benny was also seeing a special teacher to help him learn to read.

Benny was now more active in the playroom, and his play was becoming less focused. The trips across the bridge were more dangerous. The children all got sick as the blocks for the bridge became boats and floated in various directions. Children's parents were separated. There was no consistent conclusion to the play. No one ended up staying in either house. Adult figures yelled at each other, shouting directions on how to drive the car or sail the boat. One day Benny brought R2-D2 and Strange Man. He again designated R2 as the toy that Dr. Gill would use, but often Benny took R2 himself. When this occurred, R2 would always be lost, hiding in one of the rooms or looking for something he had lost. Strange Man was larger than any of the other figures. He was taking command of the trips, ordering everyone where to go. No one liked Strange Man and they called him a monster. When he was not obeyed, he threw figures off the bridge or boat and into the water. He became very angry when one of the boy figures called him a dummy. Strange Man grabbed the toy and crushed him. The figure of Strange Man became increasingly aggressive as R2 became more isolated and afraid.

Dr. Gill used the play themes to help Benny recognize that the figures of R2 and Strange Man were both sides of himself. This was difficult because Dr. Gill felt that, at this time, the family tensions and conflicts would interfere with Benny's individual work. Benny's parents' own difficulties in their relationship would limit their ability to give Benny the love and support he needed to explore his own feelings. This all came to a head with one incident. One stormy evening Sandra had made arrangements for Maria to stay with Benny while she went out. However, Maria became ill and recommended that a friend of hers, Lauda, stay with Benny. Sandra agreed. However, when Lauda arrived it was apparent that she spoke limited English. Sandra left instructions in both English and her limited Spanish. While Sandra was gone it is unclear what happened, but Dusty was let out and Lauda forgot she had put him outside. Benny was asleep when Sandra came home. She paid Lauda and then went to bed. It was after midnight when Benny woke her up and wanted to know where Dusty was. They looked for him in the house and then the yard. Dusty was gone.

Sandra and Benny spent two hours driving around in the heavy rain looking for Dusty. In the morning Benny was crying and refused to go to school. He said he had to look for Dusty. When Sandra said they couldn't because she had to go to work, Benny called her a bitch and ran out into the rain. Sandra chased him for half a block before she caught him. He fell to the ground crying and yelled he would never go back. Sandra began to cry and went to her knees and hugged him. She canceled her work day and she and Benny spent most of the day in a futile attempt to find Dusty.

Benny's play was now filled with the intense anger that had appeared in his first play sessions. Strange Man was an even more unforgiving, destructive force. Princess Lila again appeared. She and R2 were in the house and would get increasingly frightened as Strange Man walked over the bridge, roaring that he would destroy them. After the assault he would cross over the bridge to the other house where a mother and father doll tried to fortify the walls to protect themselves. As Strange Man crashed through the door, everyone ran out. In a shift in the play, Strange Man spoke to his victims saying that they deserved to die. Lila was a particular focus of anger because she never protected R2. She always left the windows and doors of the house open.

After three days they found Dusty. The postman came to the house and said he thought he had seen Dusty running in a park about a mile away. It had been raining for two days, and when they found Dusty he looked very tired and frightened. They washed him and tried to feed him. Benny was very happy, but he immediately noticed that Dusty was not himself. He wouldn't eat. He and Benny slept together that night. Sandra had called Steven, and the next morning Steven, Sandra, and Benny took Dusty to the veterinarian. Dusty had pneumonia and was very weak. They decided that he needed to stay at the clinic for treatment.

Benny's play was very disorganized, varying from times of extreme aggressive outbursts to intervals when people were adrift by themselves on boats. The boats resulted from the collapse of the bridge. R2 stayed at home in bed. He had a television set and watched programs all day. When Strange Man came into the house, Lila and everyone else ran out. Except for R2. Strange Man would go to his room, look at him, and tell him to eat. Dr. Gill had been using R2 as a spokesman for his own comments and interpretations of the play. He had been linking Strange Man's anger at people whom he needed with R2's feeling helpless and sad because of the same situation. Dr. Gill commented on Strange Man's interest in R2 and wish to take care of him. During a sequence in the play, Strange Man went to R2 and told him he had something to show him. He helped R2 out of bed and they went outside the house. Strange Man said, "Now watch this," as Benny began to deconstruct Strange Man. There were four layers to the robot that could be taken apart to reveal another robot within. As Benny transformed the robot, he talked to R2 saying that the more layers taken off, the weaker Strange Man became. Finally Benny unveiled a much smaller robot that looked almost human. He then unlocked a small door in that robot's chest to reveal a very small robot. It had essentially a human form. "That's me," Benny said as he looked from R2 to Dr. Gill.

The next morning Dr. Gill got a call from Steven. The veterinarian had told them that Dusty was not going to live. He gave him maybe two or three days. Steven asked Dr. Gill to meet with Sandra and him before they brought Dusty home. When they met, Dr. Gill was impressed by the change in Benny's parents. They were both alarmed by their son's displays of anger at them, accompanied by his clinging and then withdrawal. Benny became very upset whenever his father prepared to go home. Benny was unable to sleep, lost his appetite, and was generally irritable. Steven decided to sleep over on the couch. The focus of the exchange with Dr. Gill was their growing awareness of how they had ignored their son. Seeing him so unhappy with the illness of Dusty, they became aware of his need for them and their love for him. They were worried how Benny would react to the loss of Dusty. Dr. Gill told them that they needed to look at their feelings about loss and death, but should let Benny work through his own feeling about the loss of Dusty. It would take time. They could be models for identification and offer Benny supportive conclusions to the experience, such as religious, scientific, philosophical, or whatever personal view they had that would make sense to a six-year-old and could be a comfort to him. The important point was that Dusty's death and Benny's grief not occur in isolation but be shared with parents who would give him emotional support. Dr. Gill gave them a list of books on death and loss that were appropriate for children of Benny's age.

Over the following two days Steven and Sandra were with Benny as Dusty became progressively weaker. Both parents took turns treating Dusty. They gave him medicine and took his temperature, and tried to make him comfortable. Steven told Benny about illness and death and how they were everywhere, in people, animals, and plants. Doctors could treat illness, and sometimes they could help and sometimes they couldn't. Sandra said she was sorry for not being home the night Dusty ran away. She also added that Benny, like Dusty, needed a reliable grown up around. From the list that Dr. Gill had given her, she bought Hans Wilhelm's (1985) story about a boy who loves a dog that dies. She read *I'll Always Love You* to Benny and this became a ritual. Steven would sit nearby and Sandra would read the story to Benny. Sandra later said that they must have read the book 50 times. When Dusty died the family was there. Benny and Sandra cried and Steven became very silent. Steven and Sandra were ready to take Dusty to a pet cemetery the next day when Benny said that he would like Dusty to be buried in the yard. He and his parents wrapped Dusty in one of Benny's old baby blankets. The dog was buried in the yard, and the three of them planted blooming flowers over the grave. They made a cross with

Dusty's name on it. The cross was placed over the grave, and Benny put Dusty's collar and name tag on it. Benny continued to want Wilhelm's book read to him. After each reading he would talk about his past good times with Dusty and how he missed him.

Dr. Gill was in phone contact with Steven and Sandra during this time. It had been two weeks since he had seen Benny. During the last appointment Dr. Gill had used his role as R2 to tell Benny that he and the little figure inside Strange Man were going to be friends, since they both were having a bad time with people they loved. Maybe they would discover that they were brothers. When Benny arrived for the appointment following Dusty's death, he did not bring Strange Man or R2. He said very little to Dr. Gill and sat at a small desk looking gloomily at his hands. When Dr. Gill expressed some concerns about both Benny and Dusty, Benny just said, "I don't want to talk about it." Dr. Gill pulled out some drawing paper and crayons and put them in front of Benny on the desk. Dr. Gill began to draw some people in a house. Benny began drawing with Dr. Gill. As they drew, Benny began to talk. There was mutual stimulation between the two as both drew pictures and told a story. There was a storm with rain that went through the windows and doors of the house. The people in the house tried to close the windows and doors, but a dog got out and ran down what looked like a road. He got hungry and tried to come home but fell off the road into water. Benny drew a boat with stick figures. There were people in the boat who rowed and rowed but couldn't find the dog.

They had used up a half-dozen sheets of paper and were past the hour when Benny put down his crayon. He told Dr. Gill that his mom and dad tried to make people feel better but that sometimes it didn't work. He said that Dusty had a doctor, and he couldn't make Dusty any better and he died. Benny said that his father told him he was sure that there was a place like heaven for good dogs like Dusty. When Dr. Gill responded to the sadness in Benny's voice, Benny said heaven may be OK for Dusty, but he loved him and missed him. He hoped that it was sunny there and that Dusty was warm. He wouldn't see him any more because when you go to that place, you go and don't come back.

The therapy with Benny continued for almost two years. The parents finally separated and Steven soon married. Sandra had a brother who was a soccer coach in the citywide children's soccer league. He took an interest in Benny. Benny joined the soccer team, and in a short time he was an outstanding player. Sandra's brother and his girlfriend became second parents to Benny. Sandra took month-long vacations with Benny and generally had more time with him. By second grade Benny was doing well in school, although he continued to be a slow reader. After Dusty's death Benny's play evolved into complex and interrelated themes of being angry with people but not destroying them. A related theme was how hard it was to be angry with people you need and love. As Benny's own family experience became more stable and predictable, he discontinued his interest in Robo-Man. It was some time before he decided to have another dog.

At a time in development when awareness of self and ownership, exploration and acceptance of one's feelings toward others and self are major issues, Benny's emotional world was falling apart. His difficulties in consciously accepting his own impulses resulted in his creation of Strange Man for the imaginary expression of his angry wishes. The figure of R2 represented Benny's feelings of vulnerability, anxiety, and isolation. Benny's understanding of Dusty's illness and death was the result of his identification with Dusty and his own need for a reliable source of affection and protection. With the death of Dusty, Benny could no longer deal with his anger at his parents and his need for their affection and protection. As a result he demonstrated withdrawal and extreme mood swings. Dusty's death, with the help of Dr. Gill, briefly brought the family together as a unit. Benny's intense feelings about the loss of Dusty were incongruous with the reactions shown by his parents. With Dr. Gill's help, Steven and Sandra were able to be empathetic with Benny's intense reaction and help their son work through his feelings of loss and grief. As is generally true, a caring family is the best support for successful grieving in a child.

STRESS, TRAUMA, AND CHILDHOOD GRIEF

As illustrated by Benny's reaction to the death of Dusty, the child's experience and understanding of death is only partially determined by the child's psychosexual stage or level of cognitive development. Probably the two most consistent factors contributing to the child's cognitive and emotional reaction are the family support available and the levels of stress and trauma involved with the event. When the death of a sibling or parent is due to an illness, there will be an accompanying psychological stress. Illness and death alone contribute to stress because they disrupt the family routine, relationships, and affective-interpersonal support systems needed by the child. The child's anxieties about death and loss also create stress. When the death is abrupt and due to an accident, suicide, or homicide, the psychological stress is complicated with trauma. These circumstances surrounding the death contribute directly to the child's successful or unsuccessful grieving. The mourning child recognizes the serious and permanent loss of the loved one. In successful grieving the child fully experiences the pain of the loss as well as the ambivalent feeling toward the sibling or parent. The previous active experience with the lost person is transformed into a memory that is psychologically satisfying and at the same time is the basis for an optimistic view of the future. Stress and trauma affect the child and the family support system and therefore can influence the grieving process.

There is no known time line for successful grieving. However, the lack of successful grieving can be recognized in the child who continues to have recurrent distressing recollections of the event and extreme reactions to any reminders of the event. Somatic complaints and recurrent disturbing dreams are common, as are irrational and enduring phobias. The memories of the lost sibling or parent are depressing and often dominated by the morbid details of the circumstances of the death. These memories usually generate anxiety and depression rather than reduce them. Both compensatory memory and imagination are lost to the traumatized child, because of the chronic prevalence of morbid, anxiety-laden images that are the result of extreme stress and trauma. This psychological state will affect the child's grieving process as well as the grieving process in the child's caregivers (Cohen et al., 2002). Parents' response to the loss of a spouse or a child can result in a number of reactions that can interfere with the remaining child's successful grieving. Parents may change their usual ways of responding to the child because of their own grief, anxiety, and anger, and consequently will be poor models for coping with the event. Frequently the parents or remaining parent actively prohibit or discourage any discussion of the meaning of the loss to the family. With the loss of one child, parents can become overprotective of the remaining child or children. This can result in the child feeling that the world is unsafe and establish a chronic need to have the security of parental protection. The parent may over-identify with the child's pain and grief with the result that the normal family boundaries and routines are changed. The child's normal bedtimes are changed and may now be a function of his or her own decision about sleeping with the caregiver. This reinforces the feeling that the parent is no longer a consistent source of control and protection. The effect of traumatic loss related to being an observer of a painful terminal illness or of a death by accident, homicide, or suicide is that the child's successful grieving is compromised by the enduring anxiety-laden memories generated by the unique and sometimes abrupt circumstances of the experience of loss.

DISTURBED REACTION TO LOSS

Clinical observations indicate that guilt is a common reaction to the loss of a parent or sibling. The pain of the loss is accompanied by the child's feeling of responsibility for the death of the parent or sib (Cain et al., 1964). This can result in the child's chronic preoccupations with his or her negative thoughts and actions toward the deceased, which nourishes the guilt. Without resolution, over time this can affect the child's self-concept, resulting in a chronic sense of being unworthy and worthless. The early experiences of death can also contribute to the child's having a confused or distorted concept of illness and death, and the relationship between illness and death. In the situation of the illness and death of an older person, children often conclude that growing up or growing older means you are going to die. Another frequent childhood distortion is that you will die at the same age as the older sib or parent. Related to this distortion is the identification of the surviving child with the deceased sibling. The child feels he or she will die at the same age or time and in the same way. Identification with the lost sibling can also be encouraged when the parents, either consciously or unconsciously, substitute the child as a replacement for the child they lost. Unfortunately, the expectations of the surviving child are based on the idealized memory of the lost child. The substitution and idealization of the lost child by the parent, combined with the guilt felt by the surviving child and his or her own idealization of the lost sib, may have enduring effects on the child's psychological development.

CHANGING THE MEMORIES OF LOSS

There are a number of clinically accepted evaluation and treatment procedures for childhood grief. Some are especially focused on children's traumatic grief (Cohen et al., 2002), others on more general evaluations of childhood traumatic grief within the context of the family structure and related issues such as available support networks (Steinberg, 1997). When the child's experience of death and loss involves post-traumatic reactions, these interventions should be considered. The focus of this text is on the effect of the child's earlier conflicted psychological history with the lost parent or sibling and the effect of the repression of those preoperational images on imagination and memory. In unsuccessful grieving, this results in a restriction in the development of imagination and, eventually, memory. The child's images, perceptions, fantasies, and memories are organized by the anxiety of loss and consequently serve compensatory functions protective of self. This restrictive preoccupation with death and loss may enrich the evocative memories surrounding the event, but they also limit the individual's imaginative range and the capacity for affective reciprocity in personal relationships. It is assumed that these images and thoughts of the past have a symbolic meaning that will tell the psychological story of the child or the adult who has experienced unsuccessful grieving. If the therapist can see the meaning in these symbols and can help the child or adult become conscious of them, the connection between imagination, memory, and current experience can be made and anxiety reduced. There are a variety of useful imagery and fantasy techniques for evaluating and treating the child who is experiencing unsuccessful grieving. The advantage of all these approaches is that, because the full meaning of the experience of loss is unconscious, the child may not be able to deal directly with the experience. Imagination and fantasy may serve as a less anxiety-laden method for explaining the child's conflicts.

As observed in the play therapy with Benny, there are times when the child may not be inclined to express current preoccupations through play. The therapist should be prepared to use other methods for expression and communication. Dr. Gill used drawing. Drawing can be used in more structured ways for evaluation purposes such as the House-Tree-Person (Hammer, 1980), or less structured approaches such as asking the child to draw pictures of people or the family. When this approach is used in therapy, the therapist can provide some direction to the content, as did Dr. Gill when he began the drawing activity by drawing the house. Children frequently can use the drawing as a way of telling their story. The activity of drawing itself seems both to focus the child's attention and reduce the affect involved in symbolically experiencing the event. If the therapist is appropriately trained or skilled, various media can be used therapeutically. The experience of death and loss can also be explored through multimedia projects (Wadeson, 2002). The child can make clay figures of friends, family members, or the deceased sibling or parent. These figures can be used in stories either directly or indirectly related to the experience. The activity helps develop a therapeutic relationship while the story provides the child with a medium for catharsis, resolution, and, eventually, successful grieving.

Projective techniques, such as the Children's Thematic Apperception Test (Bellak & Bellak, 1950) and the Rorschach (Rorschach, 1942), have considerable histories as useful procedures for the clinical evaluation of children. One limitation of these procedures is the lack of a reliable scoring system that has some clinical use and validity with children. When used with children, the procedures can elicit images and precepts that may reveal unconscious preoperational themes related to the experience of death and loss. Research using a divergent thinking scoring method and an affect-in-play scale demonstrated that second-grade children expressing primary process thinking on the Rorschach also engaged in more affective expression in their play and were generally more comfortable in the play environment (Russ & Grossman-McKee, 1990). In an attempt to integrate the developmental theories of Piaget and Freud, Young and Fast (1985) developed a scoring system that is sensitive to the levels of psychological differentiation represented in a response to the Rorschach inkblot. Cognitive egocentrism is demonstrated in the preoperational child who has yet to differentiate between that which is thought about and the process of thinking that is attributed to self. The persistence of such egocentric thinking is represented in the Rorschach response in which the individual does not attempt to justify the response or aspects of the response by reference to the actual configuration of the blot. The scoring system reflects the subject's capacity and commitment in making such integration. Another dimension of egocentrism measured by the scoring system is omnipotence. Omnipotence is conceptualized as the child's early sense that existence is a function of her or his own experience. The development of this cognitive state is observed as the child begins to make the distinction between events that she or he can or cannot control and the correlated awareness of the self as a center of intention that is modified by interaction with causality. In the Rorschach, omnipotence is represented by indications that the individual does not demonstrate an adequate awareness that the inkblot is simply an inkblot but is responded to as a configuration that has some meaning or intention. The individual must "figure out" what the inkblot means.

At this time, this scoring system has been applied in clinical studies with adults and demonstrates satisfactory statistical qualities for classifying and understanding deviant responses to the Rorschach. Anxiety and consequent repression could disrupt the expected development of both cognitive egocentrism and omnipotence. With modification the scoring system might prove to be useful for evaluating relationships between levels of egocentric thought, imaginative content, and reactions to anxiety-generating experience for children, such as death or loss. However, as is true of the other projective techniques discussed, the clinical use of the Rorschach is limited by the absence of a scoring system established by relevant developmental content that would aid in the clinical interpretation of the child's projective responses. The clinical application of projective techniques to evaluate the imagery and fantasies of children is thus greatly dependent on the clinical sensitivity and skills of the clinicians who use them.

CHILDHOOD IMAGINATION AND PLAY THERAPY

Grief resolution in children can be interrupted when the conditions of loss are confounded with extreme stress and trauma. As a consequence the child demonstrates anxiety, depression, preoccupations, and difficulties in relationships. In these situations, treatment models may use group therapy to address the specific psychological reactions that are the result of extreme stress or trauma or both (Cohen et al., 2002). Individual cognitive behavior therapy may be the treatment of choice for the child experiencing traumatic grief. Bereavement-focused cognitive behavior therapy includes work with the child's fantasies and images. Similar techniques are used in a model that is suitable for children who are experiencing bereavement not associated with extreme stress or trauma (Martin & Williams, 1990). Therapeutic interventions with a specific focus on imagery that could prove useful in working with a child experiencing unsuccessful grieving include relaxation therapy, systematic desensitization, guided affective imagery, mindplay, and movement and drama therapy (Singer, 1993).

Play therapy uses the child's relationship with the therapist and an exploration of the metaphorical themes expressed in the symbols of play to help the child experience successful grieving. The assumption is that, through play, the child will express and explore conflicted feelings that result from ambivalent feelings toward the lost family member and remaining family members that cannot be consciously explored. Because the child senses that these images and fantasies are incongruous with the feelings expressed by psychologically important family members, the therapy requires appropriate collateral supportive interventions with the family. Through the child-therapist relationship and interpretations of the story told in the play, the therapist helps the child come to a conscious awareness of his or her full range of feelings toward the lost family member and important members of the existing family. As our case story demonstrated, Benny's understanding of the loss of Dusty, and his successful grieving, were the result of his relationship with Dr. Gill and the support provided by his parents. Through supportive family work, the therapist can help the family unit experience successful grieving. In the next chapter, as we turn to the story of Tyrone and Lucas, it will become apparent that the loss of a brother and movement toward successful grieving involve psychological processes similar to those for Benny and Dusty.

CHAPTER 4

Playing with Magic

I wish you would go away!
Tyrone, Age 8

Tyrone, an African-American boy, was born in a small rural town in the deep South. The family was very poor, and Tyrone's father apparently left the family when Tyrone was less than a year old. The history of his early life is not well known, but some time after the father left, Tyrone and his mother, Vernez, and two older sisters moved in to live with her mother. That home was small, and a number of the grandmother's own children and grandchildren lived in close quarters and shared bedrooms. His "uncle" Lucas, who was four years older than Tyrone, was already living in the house when Tyrone arrived. Again, the history is unclear, but Lucas may have been his half-brother through an earlier relationship of his mother's. The grandfather had been dead a number of years, and the grandmother's brother was the minister of the local Pentecostal Church. The one thing that the family shared was the faith strengthened by attendance at the church services. These were emotional experiences, and Tyrone sometimes witnessed his mother and grandmother as they were possessed by the spirit and spoke in different voices.

By the time Tyrone was four or five, he and Lucas were close companions in a home that consisted mainly of females. They went to the same school together. However, in the father's absence, Lucas was treated by Vernez more as a companion and peer than as a young boy. He was accepted as the authority in the house when the older women were gone or busy, and he was allowed to discipline some of the girls who were his age and older. There was evidence that physical punishment was used by the mother, grandmother, and the growing Lucas as a means of discipline. By the time Lucas was ten, he was a tall, husky boy who was the size of his aunt (or mother) and grandmother.

The local school had a basketball court, and it was here that most of the young black males spent their time. In this small town, basketball was a major pastime for boys, and the local high school often had a basketball team in the state tournament. Lucas was soon known for his skill in basketball and was often chosen by the older boys to play on their team. Tyrone was a good player for his age but couldn't measure up to Lucas. Both boys enjoyed the game and would spend time playing one-on-one almost every day in the summer. The games were very competitive, and sometimes Tyrone's mother complained that Lucas was too rough on her son.

When Tyrone was eight and Lucas was twelve, the boys, Vernez, and her two daughters moved from the rural South to a large city on the East Coast to live with a brother of Vernez. The event was abrupt, and the family moved into a crowded apartment in the low-income projects. The projects were a large complex; most of the families living there were black and on some sort of state or federal support. In their previous home the family had known almost everyone in town, but here they had their immediate family and no one else. The schools were much larger and had to be reached by bus. Lucas began to miss school, and within three months of the move he was identified as a behavior problem. There was a basketball court near the apartment, and Tyrone and Lucas spent much of their spare time at the court. The pick-up games were much more physical than back home, and the boys imitated the black basketball stars they saw on television. There was a custom that the better players got nicknames of the professional stars. It was a mark of a boy's status in the group. Lucas was soon called "Magic" after Magic Johnson.

About six months after the move, Lucas did not go to school one day and disappeared. Vernez called the police after three days. Tyrone thought Lucas had gone back to his grandmother's. He told his mother that he and Lucas had talked about going back together. His mother was very angry with Tyrone, as if he in some way had caused the disappearance of Lucas. Two days after the police had been contacted, Lucas was found naked, floating face down in a nearby abandoned reservoir. The coroner said that he had drowned and estimated that he had been dead about five days. For some time there was speculation that Lucas may have been kidnapped and murdered. The circumstance of his death was in the newspaper, with a picture of a smiling, handsome Lucas. The speculation went on for almost a month, when the father of a neighborhood boy told the police that Lucas had been swimming in the reservoir with his son and two or three other boys when he simply went underwater and never came up. The boys had ignored a "no trespassing" sign and climbed over the fence that surrounded the city property.

Vernez was devastated. Because of the condition of the body, she was discouraged from seeing Lucas, but she insisted. This resulted in her total collapse and need for sedation. The local Pentecostal Church was active in supporting the family. A closed-coffin funeral was held in the church after Vernez was able to attend. The neighbors in the projects also helped to support the devastated family.

Tyrone had missed almost a month of school during this crisis. When he returned, the teachers observed that he was quiet and withdrawn. Whereas before everyone knew that Tyrone loved lunchtime, he now seldom ate. The teachers felt that he was often close to tears, and one day during recess a teacher found him crying, off in a corner of the school yard by himself. Kneeling down and holding his hand, she asked him what was wrong. Tyrone replied that he and his mother were seeing Lucas every other night and that Lucas was asking him to come and see him in heaven.

Tyrone was seen by the principal and school counselor. During these interviews he remained tearful and upset while maintaining the same story. Someone asked how he would get to heaven to see Lucas, and he matter-of-factly replied that he could take some pills or go to the reservoir and drown himself. Vernez was interviewed, and during a very emotional exchange with the school psychologist, she said she also wanted to join Lucas in a "better place." Vernez was referred to a local outpatient community mental health clinic. Tyrone, because of his suicide risk and stressful home environment, was referred and admitted to a children's inpatient psychiatric unit for further evaluation. This event made Tyrone even more anxious and depressed. Vernez had agreed to the hospitalization, and the family visited Tyrone. This was the first separation of Tyrone and his family, and he expressed his unhappiness.

Tyrone had been assigned to Charles, a young, white child psychiatry resident. During the course of the interviews with Vernez and the rest of the family, it became clear to Charles that in the isolated, rural part of the South where generations of the family had been born and raised, spirits of the dead often came to visit the living relatives. As was true with Lucas, the spirits were seldom frightening but were comforting and informative about how things were in the afterlife. For example, Lucas had told Vernez and Tyrone that the drowning was not so bad and that he was OK now. He missed them.

Charles saw Tyrone in play therapy. Tyrone told Charles that the only time he saw Lucas was at night when his mother had come into his room. Lucas's empty bed was there, and she would sit or lie there until she told Tyrone that Lucas was in the bed or in the room. As part of the evaluation, Tyrone was seen for projective testing, by Dareen, a staff psychologist. On the Rorschach, Tyrone was very cautious in expressing his imagination. He essentially gave the more common responses to the inkblots, and he seldom went beyond the form provided by the blot itself. However, his responses did not express overwhelming anxiety, intrusive thoughts, or marked preoccupations. There were expressions of dependency and some depression. This depression was also expressed in the stories Tyrone told to the Children's Apperception Test. In Tyrone's stories, children could not rely on adults, who seemed as helpless as they were. For example, a family was camping and a small child left the tent at night and went into the woods by himself. When the mom and dad discovered he was gone, they both went into the woods to look for him. They got separated from each other, and in the ending of the story all three family members were separated and lost.

When Tyrone told stories to Dareen about loss or death, it was clear that he was retelling his experiences of the death of Lucas. Stimulated by a picture of three figures playing tug-of-war with one figure on one end of the rope and two on the other end, Tyrone told a story in which the one figure was stronger than the other two. This figure was also smarter than the other two, but the rope broke and the lone character fell backwards into deep water and could not get out. There was no water in the picture. Presented with a card in which three young children were seated around a table eating while a rather ill-defined adult figure stood in the background, Tyrone said that the figure was a ghost. He then said that the ghost was cold and hungry and wanted breakfast. Tyrone's eyes were moist and he seemed ready to cry.

At this point Dareen put down her pencil and pad and asked Tyrone if he missed Lucas and thought about him. Tyrone spoke in a quiet voice; he wondered if Lucas was really happy in heaven. The last time he had visited Tyrone and his mother he had said he'd like to have Tyrone come and see him. Tyrone said he thought Lucas was lonely. When asked how he would get to heaven to see Lucas, Tyrone thought for a while. He said he didn't know for sure but probably he would have to die. He was now unclear how he would do that. Dareen asked in a matter-of-fact way about what he and Lucas could do in heaven. Tyrone seemed surprised at the question. He said he hadn't thought much about it. After a pause he said that they would just "hang out." Then after another pause his face lit up and he said that they would play basketball.

Every afternoon the children on the psychiatric unit were taken to the outdoor playground, which had a half-court basketball facility. Tyrone would not play in the games organized by the other boys but would often play by himself. The recreation staff was impressed by his grace on the court and the accuracy of his shots. One day Charles came out to watch him play. During the one and a half weeks that Tyrone had been on the unit, he and Charles had formed a good relationship. While Charles stood watching, Tyrone bounced the ball to him. Charles was an excellent child psychiatry resident, but he was a mediocre ball player. Tyrone saw this at once and suggested that they play a game of free throw. Tyrone had been observed before to be very accurate at the free-throw line, but now he seldom made a shot. When Charles occasionally made one, Tyrone would make a positive comment and eventually they would give each other "high fives." Tyrone asked Charles if they could play basketball rather than meet for therapy. Charles agreed, and they began playing one-on-one games. During these games the grace and accuracy at the basket that Tyrone had shown when he played by himself disappeared. He made the appearance of guarding Charles, but clearly he was allowing him every opportunity to control the ball and score.

After Tyrone was discharged from the unit, Charles continued to see him once a week in therapy in the outpatient department. Vernez brought Tyrone to therapy, and Charles saw her every other week. It was not possible to play basketball at a court, so Charles brought in a small ball and net that could be hung over the door of the playroom. The games continued for a while as they had before, with Charles always winning. Spontaneously, Tyrone began talking about Lucas with the general theme of how he missed him and how everyone, including his mother, loved him. While he and Charles played, Tyrone talked about how great a ball player Lucas was. He was as good as Magic Johnson, maybe better. If he had lived he would have gone to college and played ball and then become a professional. During the basketball games, Tyrone began calling Charles "Magic." When Charles asked Tyrone what he might call him, he replied, "just Tyrone."

The play was intense and ritualistic. Tyrone could not tolerate Charles's varying his role as Magic, and he ignored most of the comments Charles would make about the process. Charles frequently commented on how difficult it must be to play against someone who was so perfect and admired by everyone. He also attempted to explore the possibility that one might admire such a person but also dislike him at times. Sometimes Tyrone would reply with a casual "yes" to the statements.

After about two months of this play, there was a shift. It began with the introduction of a referee. Tyrone complained that Charles could always get the rebound for a missed shot because he was taller. Charles said that a referee was needed. Tyrone spontaneously took on the role by bringing a white baseball cap to the session. He would wear it turned backward during the game, but when he became the referee he positioned the cap with the brim forward, while his voice would drop into a baritone and his face would frown. Although Charles continued playing as before, Tyrone, as the referee, called him for an enormous number of fouls. The most frequent foul was "illegal use of being big and tall." The fouls resulted in Tyrone turning his hat around and shooting from the foul line. In this way Tyrone began winning games. He started to be more aggressive, both in the game and as the referee. Although as a player Tyrone seldom said anything, as he became more physical as the referee, he would make numerous comments as he called fouls against Charles. The content generally was that Charles took advantage of his age and size. Although Charles continued playing as before, the referee called fouls on him for unsportsmanlike conduct. According to the referee, he called Tyrone a "shrimp" and a "little pussy" as well as other derogatory terms.

These games continued with growing intensity. Charles had to remind Tyrone that this was play and that neither one of them would hurt the other in the playroom. Tyrone was generally able to control his aggression. Charles also began to comment that Tyrone needed a sympathetic referee to help him compete with Magic, who was a good ball player but also was bigger and made nasty remarks to him. These comments were made in the context of the game, and Tyrone began to respond to them in the play. At times Charles was Magic and at other times he was Charles, and Tyrone would respond to his comment with his own. During the game, Tyrone would tell Magic that he was a bully and unfair and that he, Tyrone, hated him. In one session while playing, Charles, as Magic, said to Tyrone, "Why do you hate me? I'm just better than you!" Tyrone replied with tremendous anger, "I wish you would go away! Just disappear!"

The session after that Tyrone arrived late and with obvious reluctance entered the playroom. He sat in a chair some distance from Charles and was silent. For a while Charles respected his silence, but finally he commented that the last ball game with Magic was pretty tough. Tyrone replied, "You made me say things that weren't true!" He said he didn't want to play basketball any more. Over the next three sessions Vernez would bring Tyrone in five to ten minutes late, and Tyrone remained mostly silent during the sessions. Charles decided to address what he thought was the issue by saying that although Tyrone loved Lucas and did miss him, there were times when he was relieved that Lucas was no longer around to say negative things about him. To Charles's surprise, Tyrone mumbled "maybe." When Charles met with Vernez the following week, she told him that she and Tyrone were moving back to live with her mother. She hated where she lived and they were moving next week.

Charles had to accept her decision but pressed to see Tyrone before they left. During their last session, Tyrone told Charles that he would miss him, but that he wanted to go back to be with his grandmother. Tyrone's mood was happy, and he spontaneously took the basketball and threw it to Charles. The game was different, and there was no referee. Tyrone became a radio announcer. The announcer said that this was the last game between the great Tyrone and the famous "Chuck." There was no mention of Magic, and every time either of them made a shot, the announcer would appropriately raise his voice in amazement at the talent of the two players. Whenever there was a score, the two would give each other high fives. Tyrone won the game.

During their last session, Vernez told Charles that Tyrone was finally going willingly to school. She admitted that she had contributed to his not going to school because she was worried that Tyrone might disappear as Lucas had. Tyrone was also beginning to play basketball at school and in the neighborhood. Neither she nor Tyrone saw Lucas any more. She remained depressed but took comfort in her church, where the pastor and a number of the members made an extra effort to let her talk about her loss and grief. Although Charles encouraged Vernez to talk with Tyrone about the loss of Lucas, she said she couldn't. Every time she tried to talk to Tyrone about Lucas, she would tear up. She said that she had never noticed before how much Tyrone and Lucas looked and acted alike. Vernez smiled slightly and said that Tyrone was so good to her. She wouldn't know how to live without his love.

Tyrone had grown up relating to Lucas as a brother-father. He found in Lucas a strong figure to identify with, although the play and some of the known history suggested that Lucas could verbally and physically abuse the younger and smaller Tyrone. Lucas obtained some of his power in Tyrone's imagination because of his exceptional skill in basketball. The stage was set for use of compensatory identification when Lucas died. The cultural and personal belief in spirits as well as the drowning added to the morbid framework for Tyrone's understanding of loss. He tried to be the "good" Lucas that his mother remembered. His difficulty with his hostile and competitive feeling toward Lucas, which was basic to his identification with Lucas's power, resulted in his difficulties in playing basketball. When he played ball with his therapist, he made Charles into the idealized Lucas, despite Charles's realistic limitation. In this contest Tyrone could not beat Lucas. The creation of the referee, who, after all, always knows the rules and the truth of the matter, allowed Tyrone for the first time to express his anger at having to play with the "Magic-Lucas" and allowed an initial attempt to explore his complex feelings about the loss of the loved and hated Lucas. The need for Vernez to have someone strong and loving to support her was accentuated by the death of Lucas. Although she was developing Tyrone into his replacement, she needed her own mother for support. Her return to her mother resulted in the disruption of Tyrone's beginning insights about self and loss.

Tyrone's experience of the death of Lucas illustrates common psychological reactions in children that, if not appropriately responded to, can result in an understanding of loss that is defined by enduring anxiety, grief, and guilt. Lucas's death occurred at a time in Tyrone's development when he was in the psychological process of becoming aware of, understanding, and eventually owning all those motivations and feelings toward people that eventually become the self. This process is mostly based on early experience with loved ones. With the death of Lucas, the remaining family members were so devastated that they were not available to help Tyrone explore his complex feelings toward a person who was now a memory. Vernez attempted to reduce her grief over the loss of Lucas by relating to Tyrone as she had toward Lucas. This common reaction of a grieving mother toward the loss of a child was also true for J. M. Barrie and Jack Kerouac. Coming to terms consciously with his more negative, competitive feelings toward Lucas generated in Tyrone interpersonal anxiety. He coped by identifying with his and the family's memory of Lucas as an idealized person now in heaven. Tyrone's conscious exploration of his negative feeling toward Lucas generated internal anxiety that could only be reduced defensively, with the consequence that unconscious processes developed generating a false sense of self.

Therapy with Charles offered Tyrone an alternative way of thinking about the death of Lucas. During the sessions, Tyrone began to make Charles into "Magic-Lucas." In a trusting relationship, in a safe environment, Tyrone began to use his imagination to retell the story of Lucas as he understood him emotionally and psychologically. It is the mark of successful therapy that history is not told by a memory dominated by the unconscious. With anxiety reduced, memory of the past can be explored and understood in terms of fuller emotional experience and a more articulate sense of self. Without such an experience, memory dominated by the unconscious will find expression in repetitious ways that might fulfill certain emotional needs but may hamper an expansion of conscious awareness of self. It is not known, but it is possible, that Tyrone's experience with Charles helped him begin a different way of remembering his past and a way to avoid repeating it.

CHAPTER 5

Dreams of Perfection

I cannot grasp all that I am.
St. Augustine (354-430)

THE INAUTHENTIC SELF

Both Benny and Tyrone were at particular developmental stages, and their caregivers in vulnerable relationships, when death and loss generated stress for both children and caregivers. The self-centered, cognitively egocentric systems of preoperational thought dominating the awareness of early experience were being transformed by more sophisticated but later-developing interacting cognitive structures. These new interrelated cognitive systems include reflective thought and the interrelated systems of language and operational thought, and these new and evolving systems result in more accurate concepts of time, space, and causality. Interrelated with these developments, but based on the emotional experience of relationships, is the evolution of self-awareness and the awareness of others. The transformation occurring during this time eventually results in an adult who has the capacity to realistically evaluate experience and access to his or her emotional life and imagination, which finds expression in enduring relationships based on emotional reciprocity and mutual satisfaction. This is an ideal state that probably is never completely obtained and is dependent on the most important development occurring during the interval: autonomous thought (Noy, 1979). Based on reflective thought, autonomous thought is conscious and relatively conflict free. Autonomous thought is basic to the give and take of interpersonal experience, because of its capacity to focus on both self and others in terms of emotions, thoughts, and motivation.

This capacity to be aware of internal states in self and others and to imagine possible outcomes from relationships can be compromised by anxiety and conflict. As observed in Benny's and Tyrone's play (Chapters 3 and 4), anxiety-laden thoughts that were incongruous with the perception of their caregivers' thoughts and motivations generated conflicts and consequently compromised behavior.

Benny's parents were so intensely involved in their own conflicts and unsatisfying relationship that they were unaware of the meaning of their son's withdrawal, sadness, and preoccupation with the sources of anger. With little emotional support from his family, who were themselves engaged in angry arguments, Benny began to have inappropriate angry outbursts and to disown his own angry feelings toward his parents. He saw himself as a mechanical monster from outer space who had tremendous powers of destruction. At the same time, he also saw himself as the inadequate droid, R2-D2, also from outer space, who was unable to cope with his own aggression, represented in the attacks of Robo-Man. Psychologically, Benny did not know where all the anger came from. Benny both loved and identified with his dog, Dusty, and the loss of Dusty resulted in too much stress. Benny's perception of his parents lack of concern for Dusty's condition resulted in severe disorganization and depression. With the help of Dr. Gill, Sandra and Steven were able to help Benny grieve for the loss of Dusty and begin to psychologically own his angry wishes and vulnerable feelings of dependency.

The situation with Tyrone was similar. Vernez was so involved in her own reaction to the loss of Lucas that she was unable to be a source of emotional support for her son. Tyrone's feelings toward Lucas before his death were ambivalent. Although he admired and identified with Lucas, he was also angry at him. The family's reaction to the loss was to produce Lucas as an idealized boy who was in heaven. For Tyrone, this was an incongruous conclusion in terms of his confused internal state. In therapy he expressed his conflicts in a basketball game that at first reflected one side of Tyrone's conflict, the idealized and powerful Lucas as portrayed by the therapist, Charles, but eventually reflected the opposite side with the help of the referee who saw Lucas as Tyrone saw him. As Tyrone began to integrate his complex feelings about Lucas, his anxiety intensified. Vernez's reaction to the loss was to reconstruct Tyrone into a Lucas-figure that she needed. Her strong dependency needs were also expressed in her move back to her mother's home. Her capacity to understand and see Tyrone as an individual was very limited. More than likely, Tyrone himself would not have a chance to imagine himself beyond the needs of his mother.

Both Benny and Tyrone had the benefits of therapy to help them become more conscious of their conflicted fantasies and feelings. When therapy is successful in helping the child sort out the conflicted representations of the past, and the child simultaneously develops reflective thought, the development of autonomous thought is possible. There are many interpersonal experiences in childhood that can produce internal anxiety and psychological defense mechanisms that limit the development of autonomous thought (Pine, 1985). The psychological consequences of these experiences for the child may be similar to those of the child who has experienced early loss and unsuccessful grieving. The differences may be in the degree of abrupt stress and trauma involved in the child's experience of death and loss, as well as the tendency to use identification with the lost individual as a defense mechanism. The child is prone to use this defense because the figure of identification is based on memory rather than experiences and is therefore a suitable figure for projective identification. Dynamic play therapy for the child who demonstrates unpleasant yet focused anxiety for relatively specific content (Pine, 1985, pp. 127-160) is similar to the play therapy for the child who has experienced unsuccessful grieving.

For the adult who develops focused anxiety as a result of unsuccessful grieving as a child, because of the absence of either appropriate family support or the opportunity for early therapeutic intervention, the psychological consequences can be profound and enduring. There is another group of adults who have experienced overwhelming general anxiety rather than event-focused anxiety early in development, with the result that their cognitive-affective development is severely disrupted and their capacity to relate to other people is limited (Pine, 1985, pp. 205-227). A major characteristic of these individuals is their difficulties in experiencing their own inner emotional states in the context of a self that is often not well defined. They may have relationships in which they have feelings of profound emptiness during a separation from the loved individual and an experience of a sense of oneness or merger in their presence. They are at times acutely aware of their thoughts and feelings, yet at other times they can be overwhelmed with their affect. While their perception and sensitivity in relations is sometimes impressive, a corresponding self-centered preoccupation expressed in idiosyncratic thoughts and fantasies is not uncommon. Their capacity to tolerate personal contact is limited, and frequently they are socially withdrawn. The problem in the integration of the self is reflected in a tendency to split their own personality into good and bad parts. Under stress they sometimes experience their own affects as due to an external source and may perceive others as the cause of both their positive and their negative feelings about themselves. Although these individuals have difficulties in relationships and in life in general, they are often productive and creative. Because of the dominance of their affective life, their imagination can be powerfully expressed in their creativity.

The important event contributing to the development of this personality may be the early experience of pronounced stress and anxiety without appropriate adult support at the time when representational and reflective thought were just developing. Because of the intense anxiety, a poorly developed discrimination between self and others, and corresponding inarticulate reflective thought, the anxiety was not a signal for repression but a sign of oncoming uncontrollable events that were threats to self (Kohut, 1959; Pine, 1985). As an adult, the individual's ability to regulate affect and reflect on self is compromised, and the experience of affect in relationships is frequently overwhelming. Relationships often serve to support a fragile sense of self and meet narcissistic demands for love. Such relationships are usually difficult to maintain. A contemporary creative individual who represents this pattern is Sylvia Plath (John-Steiner, 2000, pp. 63-97). Plath lost her father when she was eight years old. Her obsession with her memories of him dominated her intimate relationships and her creativity. The possible causes for such disruptions in early development are numerous, but the trauma of death and loss experienced early in childhood was probably crucial for Plath, as it was for Emily Brontë. Brontë's loss of her mother, at age three, occurred at a point in time when her important developmental issues were attachment to and trust in a loving mother who could, through her caregiving, be a source of satisfaction and a model for the regulation of affect (Stern, 1977; Winnicott, 1965). Soon after Brontë's birth her mother was pregnant with Anne, and after her younger sister's birth her mother died of cancer. It is doubtful that during this time she was very available to Emily or any of her six children. From ages two to six, Brontë had a rival for love, her sister Anne, and her mother figures were her other sisters who were only three and five years older than herself. In a short time, her older sisters died in the same year: Maria at age twelve and Elizabeth at age ten. At that time Emily was seven years old. As a result of this tragic history of early loss it would appear that Brontë's sense of self was fragile and her boundaries between self and others not well defined. The capacity to construct needed objects in imagination is seen in her poetry as she creates her powerful muse in the *Visitant,* and in the symbiotic love of *Wuthering Heights.* In the *Visitant,* Brontë is unclear of the source of her creativity and sees it as unreliable. Without the modulating effect of his other self, the loved, idealized, and dead Catherine, Heathcliff loses his control and is overcome with hatred and rage. Deprived of the experience of relating to and identifying with an idealized person with desirable qualities, Brontë searched for completeness in her imagination. She was never able to leave the home she was born in or the family she knew. Brontë was dominated by her emotional life and her creativity but limited in her capacity to express her feelings in her relationships.

Although dominated by their emotional life and invested in their imagination, J. M. Barrie, Isak Dinesen, and Jack Kerouac experienced loss later in their development. They were capable of leaving their home, the place where the loss of love occurred and their sense of self was established, to search for love in an experience that could fulfill a wish for a more desirable and complete sense of self. Their loss was organized within a cognitive structure where representative and reflective thought were stable enough that a sense of self and an awareness of others were evolving. However, internal anxiety experienced in the interpersonal context of early loss disrupted this process. Like Benny at the beginning of his therapy, all three authors as adults were unable to get personal satisfaction in relationships. Throughout their lives they had a difficult time owning their aggressive wishes and integrating wishes with an acceptance of their dependency needs. Benny's experience with the death of Dusty, his loved and reliable companion, and his parents' lack of awareness of the metaphorical meaning of the event for him, brought the issues into focus. In similar ways, the experience of death galvanized the relationships of Barrie, Dinesen, and Kerouac with their families. For Benny, Dr. Gill was able to help him and his family through the crisis.

The three writers of loss never had such experiences. Like Tyrone, they continued to have an idealized memory of the lost family member that served as a figure for projective identification. Tyrone's limited capacity to consciously explore his aggressive wishes toward Lucas was due to internal anxiety but also due to his mother's psychological need to have him become her memory of Lucas. This pattern encourages the development of a false self. Tyrone could not be the source of his own feelings as he became Lucas to reduce internal and interpersonal conflicts. This same psychological relationship with a depressed and dependent mother who was also grieving was experienced by both Barrie and Kerouac. The long-term results were that as adults, they were often only vaguely aware of their own wishes in their relationships with women. They tried to explore and understand what it all meant to them by creating relationships with women in stories whose meaning seemed to escape them. This was true in stories such as *Tommy and Grizel* by Barrie (1943) and *Visions of Cody* by Kerouac (1993). This effort to understand relationships by telling a story that at the same time creates a part of self that is more acceptable, while exploring that part of self that feels psychologically incomplete, is a significant motivation for writers of loss.

CREATING A SENSE OF COMPLETENESS

There is often a tension in an individual that motivates him or her to create. This creative person has enduring opposing emotions and values, and the creative act is an effort to reconcile these opposites and reduce the tension. The tensions are often generated by the emotions and anxieties of childhood. The creative individual, in telling his or her story, tries to capture the essence of the event and in the process reactivate the pain. The anxiety experienced by the child was overwhelming, but now under the control of an adult imagination, the pain is manageable and to some degree understandable. Whereas, before, the memory created a disequilibrium in the sense of self, in the process of writing a sense of wholeness is momentarily established. The process of writing itself may involve both pleasurable and unpleasurable memories and affects, but when successful the author has a sense of mastery and pleasure. However, this process frequently does not result in a significant and enduring reduction in tension. Writing about anxiety-producing events, whether they be recent or in the past, may have a short-term emotionally satisfying cathartic function but may not result in an increased understanding. Repeating the story is self-satisfying and self-serving, but without some outside source that provides a change in perspective, the individual's sense of past and self does not change (Marlow & Wagner, 1991). The situation is similar to the person who talks things over again and again but doesn't want any feedback. There has to be a relationship where the other person serves to help the individual understand the memory and the tensions that remain a source of current dissatisfaction.

Many sources of conflicted childhood memories can serve as a motivation to create, but the relationship to early loss in childhood of either a parent (Albert, 1971) or a sibling (Pollack, 1978) is certainly remarkable. The association has been noted and variously explained (Schultz, 1996), but the reason for the association is best explained by the enduring effects of unsuccessful grieving in the surviving child that results in the developmental arrest of representational, reflective, and autonomous thought (Noy, 1979). The development of an awareness of the mental process in self and others is intimately linked and is basic to the development of social awareness and social interaction. The child's capacity to know that others have thoughts and motivations has been studied extensively. These studies demonstrate that beginning at age two, children evolve an increasing articulate awareness of how their own cognitive and emotional processes interrelate with similar processes in other children and adults (Butterworth et al., 1991). By age five, children demonstrate that they have a psychic life that can be influenced by the content of other people's thought and motivation. Reflective thought evolves from interpersonal experience and is crucial to the development of self-evaluation and an understanding of broader social realities that exist beyond the individual's immediate experience.

The ability to reliably consider that others may have thoughts, feelings and motivations that may be similar to one's own or may differ from one's own is basic to social interaction. This capacity signals the decreasing dominance of egocentric thought with its self-centered limitations. An unstable capacity in this domain is associated with severe psychological disorders such as autism (Barren-Cohen, 1991) and borderline pathology (Fonagy, 1989). Early interpersonal experience generating internal anxiety, when emerging but unacceptable thoughts become the subject of reflective thought, can contribute to the disruption of the ability to reliably observe self and others. Under these psychological conditions, thoughts about self and others are not autonomous. Consequently, the ability to understand people as they are is confounded by the individual need to see and relate to them based on one's own unconscious motivations—as Tyrone did with Charles. In the realm of imagination Tyrone in essence created Charles as a figure based on his unconscious conflict rather than developing an awareness of Charles as an independent figure with his own thoughts and emotions. In the context of play therapy, Charles became Lucas for Tyrone, and Charles as the therapist used Tyrone's fantasies to understand these conflicts. The goal in this model of therapy is that eventually Tyrone might be able, under conditions of reduced anxiety and greater interpersonal trust, to come to a more conscious awareness of his own thoughts and motivations. In the process, both reflective and autonomous thought could be available for the continued development and life-long elaboration of self and awareness of others.

Frequently, the psychological outcome of unsuccessful grieving in the adult is the repetitious attempt to explore and define self in relationships that are attempts to understand and change a confusing childhood memory of loss that made a part of the self isolated and unknown. Emily Brontë had been the caretaker of her failed and drug-addicted brother, Branwell, when she began the story of Heathcliff. As a child she could not control or master death. As a loving sister she tried to support and protect her self-destructive brother from death. Soon after Branwell's death, Brontë withdrew, refused to eat or leave the house, and in three months she followed Branwell. J. M. Barrie was in the middle of a marriage that was a threat to his definition of himself as a mature sexual male and his sense that he was only a boy, when he met the five-year-old George Davies in Kensington Gardens and, figuratively and literally, created and related to him as the child he needed rather than the child that George was. Barrie was to seek out and write about these young boys of his imagination all his life. He had difficulty knowing how to relate to them as they grew up. Isak Dinesen attempted to create and relate to men who were her fantasy of her idealized yet suicidal father. In her two most significant relationships, her need to perceive the men based on her own needs rather than on their needs resulted in both men distancing themselves from the relationship. When she told her story of her love affair with Denys Finch-Hatton, it was a romantic memory concluding with his death. At the time he was actually in the process of leaving her. Finally, Jack Kerouac's relationships with William Burroughs, Neal Cassady, and Gary Snyder reflected his creation of a wished-for father figure who could protect and accept him, in the case of Burroughs, and an idealized and lost brother, in the case of Cassady and Snyder.

The failure to grieve and to come to some satisfying conclusion about what the early loss meant to the adult over-determines that individual's perception of self and consequently his or her perception of other people. Imagination is restricted because of the restrictions on reflective thought and the limited range of autonomous thought. At the same time the individual's intense memory of the past, and the need to understand or reconstruct it, results in elaborate variations of that past. There is a chronic fascination with a past that continues to generate an intensity of feelings that is almost as great as those experienced at the time of loss. In relationships these individuals have a limited capacity to understand the thoughts and feelings of others, because they can only relate to the loved person from their memories of the past and the need to have a relationship that mitigates both a false sense of self and a sense of incompleteness. Although a major weakness in the establishment of a fulfilling relationship, this need to repeat the past is a major strength for the writer of loss. Such writers feel that their past contains a truth about their existence that they only vaguely understand. In the interrelated process of retelling the story and by repeating relationships, they attempted to establish the truth of the matter. In the process they created stories of bigger-than-life heroes and heroines who may be vulnerable to death but are not intimidated by it.

For Emily Brontë, J. M. Barrie, Isac Dinesen, and Jack Kerouac, their understanding of experience, ability to relate to others, and use of imagination may have been overdetermined by their experience of early loss and unsuccessful grieving. Their creativity may also be related to that experience. But their early experience of loss may have also exposed them earlier and more intensely to an awareness of the universality of death. The writers of loss possessed an existential awareness early in life of the possibility that life is meaningless, and experienced the anxiety generated by knowing that the death that changed their life was also to be part of their future (Vanderberg, 1991). The early experience of loss occurred before more internal and social systems of thought that could have created some psychological space from the event were available for understanding. The conditions of knowing were determined by the preoperational fantasies of the self-centered child. Because of lack of differentiation between self and others, the death of the sibling or the parent was their death. The event was barely known by external social systems but rather by egocentric thought and a poorly articulated capacity to reflect on that thought. For the child, the death of a psychologically important pet or person is experienced on a much more immediate personal basis than for an adult. The immediacy of the experience serves to construct a memory that uniquely organizes later adult experience. As Kerouac expressed it, the death of his brother, Gerard, was the beginning of the mysteries. The writers of loss understood that the mystery and finality of death was central to their experience of life and that a meaningful existence might be generated by the psychological mastery of death through intense involvement in relationships, creativity, and experience. Death was important to them because it defined through negation what it meant for them as survivors to exist. In this way their own early experience and developing awareness of the uncertainty about the meaning of human experience made them existentialists.

Childhood play and adult creativity can be an effort to master past traumatic events (Cohen et al., 2002; Freud, 1961). But childhood play and adult creativity can also be understood as a way of comprehending the past and expressing a wish for the future. Play and writing as expressions of imagination reflect the past but also project how experience and life can be. From this wish comes the effort for the writer of loss not to repeat the past but to imagine a different, idealized, and romantic future. In their major works, a sense of psychological truth is explored in events that establish realities about self with the uncovering of this sensed psychological truth. The discoveries often demonstrate the limited possibilities of the original, poorly articulated, romanticized idea. Characters may be transformed by the experience, but elaboration of the psychological truth of the matter does not always result in a positive epiphany of self-revelation. At the end of the story, the characters seem as if they would continue down the same path given a similar opportunity. Heathcliff can obtain love and know himself only through death. Peter Pan concludes that he can never grow up and never obtain mature love. Dinesen's aged Pellegrina finally admits that her pursuit of love was self-centered and destructive to the person she loves. Kerouac discovers that the Great Snake that has pursued him since childhood is part of himself, but he cannot change his sense of being guilty and unworthy.

Perhaps the enduring appeal of these writers to the reader is that the important psychological core of their existence remained a mystery to them; yet they were compelled to pursue its meaning. This is a common psychological experience, and the art of these writers' stories comes in part from their capacity to create both fictional characters with whom the reader can identify and an emotional sense of place that the reader can imagine. The individuals in the stories have the stamp of the writer's personality, and they speak to the reader's own undiscovered and poorly understood parts of self. The reader's own recollection of a special place and a past experience intimately related to a poorly understood memory is evoked by the descriptions of the Moors, Neverland, the farm in Africa, and Dean Moriarty's superfast 1949 Hudson in *On the Road.* Because these storytellers knew they had experienced something important, they knew they had a story to tell.

CHAPTER 6

Emily Brontë and Her Visitant: Lost Love and Creativity

Speak God of Visions, plead for me
And tell why I have chosen thee!
Emily Brontë (1818-1848)

Emily Brontë's process of romantic ideation differs from that of J. M. Barrie, Jack Kerouac, and Isak Dinesen: instead of searching for another person to make herself whole, she turned to Nature as the muse for her creative powers. The "God of Visions" in Brontë's poem is inextricably bound to Nature as well as to herself. She believed that a powerful unity existed between her creative powers and Nature. It is this level of cognition that will formulate the basis for her poetry and her mystic experience. Perhaps it was her counter-phobic response to this power that led to this identity. It began in her childhood. She was six years old when she experienced the violence of a sudden storm upon the moors of Haworth. The earth trembled; the torrent of rain created mud slides as the peaty subsoil roared down the hillside; water and wind combined to hurl boulders from the heights into the valley. Brontë and her companions, out on the moors, were in the middle of this natural debacle. Lashed by the driving storm, they took shelter at a nearby farm building, where they viewed this wild cataclysm. Clearly, the young Emily was awed and delighted; later she would be addicted to storms, contemptuous of those persons who were frightened by them (Gérin, 1971). It was as if Nature had produced this drama especially for her; the narcissism of Brontë's preoperational thought is paramount as we see her identify with the power of Nature.

This passion for Nature was accepted by her father, the Reverend Patrick Brontë, who, sharing his daughter's feelings, frequently exempted her from the responsibilities of church attendance and religious teaching on Sundays. Emily worshiped on the moors. Later she would incorporate the power and beauty she experienced in this cosmic setting into her poetry. Frequently, the aspects of Nature in her poems become themes rather than setting. Thus, the

Yorkshire setting of Haworth becomes a paramount force in Emily Brontë's life and creativity.

Patrick Brontë also extolled the beauties of the physical world in his poetry. It was the great bond between them. That her father used the vehicle of poetry to express his feelings is also significant to Emily's creativity. She must have read her father's poetry, published in two volumes: *Cottage Poems* (1811) and *The Rural Minister* (1813). His books were displayed in local bookshops, as well as on the shelves of the Brontë parsonage. Emily demonstrated a variety of talents at an early age; she could draw and paint as well as write. Her decision to use poetry as the expression of her deepest, personal feelings indicates some emulation of this parent who shared her worship of Nature; he was the sole parent she would know.

When Emily was two years old, her father moved his family to Haworth Parsonage, a two-story early Georgian building, situated at the top of a hill, at the edge of the Yorkshire Moors. Adjacent to the house was an old cemetery through which a path led to the Brontë church and Rev. Brontë's congregation. This became Emily's world. One year later her mother, Maria, died at age 38 from cancer; she left six children whom she had borne in the past seven years. Death was no stranger to the parsonage at Haworth. While the three-year-old Emily did not remember her mother or her death, she was six when her two eldest sisters, Maria and Elizabeth, died from tuberculosis at the ages of twelve and ten. Since their mother's death, Maria had functioned as a substitute mother for all the children, and her loss was strongly felt by the family, especially by Charlotte and Branwell, ages nine and eight. It was Branwell who swore that he heard Maria's voice crying outside the window at night, begging to be let in from the cold (Bentley, 1969).

Emily Brontë never forgot that image. It reappears years later as the spirit of the dead Catherine Earnshaw, pleading at the windows to enter Wuthering Heights. "Let me in! Let me in! . . . It's twenty years . . . I've been a waif for twenty years" (Brontë, 1960, p. 25). It is significant that this spirit of Catherine, who died as an adult, shows itself as a child to Lockwood, a visitor to Wuthering Heights. His vicious response to this child, rubbing its wrist on the broken pane of glass till the blood soaked the bedclothes, denotes his absolute terror because Lockwood is a moral, rational man.

Besides the fear, the terror of the Brontë siblings, there was anger. Charlotte, even as a child, could not reconcile the extraordinary goodness of her sisters with their punishment by death. The portrait of Maria is found as Helen Burns in *Jane Eyre.* What evolved within a year of the older Brontë sisters' deaths was a regrouping of the remaining four children—Charlotte (ten), Branwell (nine), Emily (eight), and Anne (six)—into a close family structure. Isolated from society geographically, psychologically, and socially, they became each others' exclusive companions as they shared their paracosms (Silvey & MacKeith, 1988).

The maternal losses were replaced by Elizabeth Branwell, older, unmarried sister of the dead mother, who left Penzance to care for the children at Haworth. It was not a happy arrangement for any of them. The aunt was stern and demanding, and the children were constantly torn between their will and hers. Clearly the world at Haworth with its tragic losses seemed out of control.

It was Charlotte who became the "mother"; it would be her role for the rest of their lives. From infancy until age 13, Emily shared a bed with Charlotte, until her sister left the parsonage for school at Roe Head. The two of them created "Bed Plays"; Charlotte tells us, "Bed Plays mean secret plays" (Gérin, 1971, p. 18).

This secrecy found in "Bed Plays" is demonstrated in the size of their manuscripts. They used minute folded sheets of paper 2 inches by 1½ inches in size. These tiny pages were stitched neatly together to form miniature books. The hand printing on these diminutive pages is so small that it is very difficult to read. Accidentally finding one of these little books, their father provided them with a normal-sized exercise book, with the admonition, "All that is written in this book must be in a good, plain, and legible hand. P.B." (Bentley, 1969, p. 33). The exercise book remained empty. Clearly, they wanted secrecy. Later, when they created the paracosm of Glasstown, it was for *them;* it was not to be shared with adults.

Patrick Brontë inadvertently became the catalyst for the children's paracosm of Glasstown. He brought home a box of wooden soldiers for Branwell and a model village for the three girls. Each child claimed a soldier and named him appropriately: Buonaparte for Branwell, Duke of Wellington for Charlotte, Gravey for Emily (he looked grave), and Waiting Boy for Anne. Each soldier had his own kingdom, for which Branwell drew the maps. This merged into the "Great Glasstown Confederacy," which embraced all the components of a real world, except that it was ruled by the Four Genii: Tallii, Branii, Emmii, and Annii. They made drawings and maps, wrote stories and plays, and dramatized what they wrote.

Glasstown became the chief preoccupation of their life as the young Genii used their magical powers to restore and to destroy life under their domain. This is all documented by Charlotte and Branwell (Fraser, 1988, p. 49). Paracosms provide compensation: thus the four Brontë children did not perceive themselves in the context of the real world as motherless and living in poverty, nor did they feel socially deprived. What they had—the companionship of one another and the richness of their creations—gave them a sense of being very special, of carrying powers within themselves that far exceeded the ordinary. Their difficulties surfaced later when some of them turned from their paracosms to the real world. They shared Glasstown for five years; it came to an end when Charlotte left for school. However, the paracosms would continue.

During these five years of play, Emily Brontë frequently portrayed the "hero" of their stories and plays. Even at a young age, Emily was the tallest, the darkest, and the most agile of the four. Her long legs enabled her to climb trees better and to run faster than Branwell, much to his chagrin. Later it would be Emily whom Patrick Brontë taught to fire the family revolver, a custom he observed each morning; Emily, who would choose a field hawk for her bird and a gigantic mastiff, Keeper, as her dog, whom she would punish with her bare fists when necessary, bloodying his eyes and then gently nursing him back to health. It should also be noted, and Charlotte documented everything, that not once in Emily's life did she express any sexual interest in or romantic affection toward a human male. While Charlotte and Anne later experienced the emotions of romantic love with men, Emily remained disdainful of the entire process. Yet she, too, later experienced romantic love and romantic ideation with her Visitant and recorded her emotions in her poetry. As for human males, there were two men in Emily's life: Patrick and Branwell Brontë, the sources for part of her masculine identity.

Now at age 13, Emily would embark on a new discovery. When Charlotte left for school, it was painful for Emily. Since infancy, not a day had been spent without Charlotte, nor had Emily slept one night without her. As Emily turned in on herself for resources, she created a new paracosm, the Kingdom of Gondal, which she shared with Anne. The paracosm of Gondal became a way of life for the sisters; they shared its secrets for the rest of their lives. Since they knew their world so intimately, perhaps they never wrote down many of the episodes, or perhaps after Emily's death Charlotte destroyed them, for none of the original manuscripts of Gondal exist (Gérin, 1971). Gondal, a land peopled by defiant characters constantly fighting for their independence, focused on feminine power: beautiful, courageous young women who engaged in exotic adventures—even imprisonment in dungeons—and never lost their spirit or wit. Emily could project her own characteristics into the Gondal heroines and control their behavior. This compensatory paracosm became such an exciting contrast to her life in the parsonage that it began to absorb her entire consciousness.

A critical component of Gondal is its setting: the Yorkshire Moors of Haworth itself. Emily found a power and beauty in this bleak landscape that she also incorporated into her poetry—not as a setting but as major themes. With Charlotte's absence came an intensification of her feelings for Nature, a merging with cosmic elements. This is coupled with a fresh knowledge of her own creative powers as she transforms the Yorkshire landscape into her kingdom of Gondal. It is a major step in Emily Brontë's search for self: Nature provides her with the medium for self-discovery and also offers her compensation from the social world from which she had retreated.

In one of Brontë's early poems, her definition of time and personal experience expresses her need to explore these beautiful images of Nature: this was her reality.

Tell me, tell me, smiling child
What the past is like to thee?
"An Autumn evening, soft and mild
With a wind that sighs mournfully."

Tell me, what is the present hour?
"A Green and flowery spray
Where a young bird sits gathering its power
To mount and fly away."

And what is the future, happy one?
"A sea beneath a cloudless sun;
A mighty, glorious, dazzling sea
Stretching into infinity."
(Hatfield, 1941, p. 30)

Brontë used her imagination to protect herself, not to explore aspects of a differentiated self. Compensatory thought was greater than adaptive thought. For it is clear that Brontë did indeed retreat from her social world outside the parsonage. Taciturn by nature, she would not acknowledge people, even in the local shops she was patronizing. It was on the moors that she escaped the stress of social convention. Here her childlike narcissism bloomed. On the eve of Brontë's seventeenth birthday, her idyllic sojourn ended when Charlotte returned to Roe Head as a teacher, and part of her salary included taking a sister as a pupil at the school; Emily was the reluctant recipient. Once more she and Charlotte would share a bed and those intimate nocturnal conversations, but it was not enough. The two sisters did not see each other at any other time, and Emily's response to the rigid routines of both work *and* play began to drain her spirit. Even on Sundays she was confined to keeping in step with the student beside her as they walked across the fields to the church—no running across the moors or scrambling up rocks.

For ten years Emily Brontë had not left the parsonage, and now this assault on her personal freedom was more than she could bear. There was no time for Gondal, and no one with whom to share it. Her sagging spirit touched her body: she grew pale, lost weight and strength; only Charlotte knew the cause of Emily's illness. Fearing that Emily would die if she didn't get home soon, Charlotte wrote to their father, begging him to recall Emily. Once home, Emily rapidly recovered in both body and spirit. The whole ordeal had lasted less than three months. Psychologically, Emily was fragile; 13 years later she would demonstrate this same capacity to destroy her body with her broken spirit.

Emily Brontë's failure to function in the real world drove her back to her world of Gondal with renewed vigor and passion. Like a child who uses play as compensation and to strengthen self-esteem, she found both in her creative power to control the fates of the incredible characters and cosmic settings. Now Emmii was the sole genie of her paracosm. Anne had replaced her as a pupil at Roe Head, and for the next two years Emily would have her liberty to explore and create.

Perhaps it was Emily Brontë's mortification over leaving Roe Head that provided the motivation for her to accept a teaching position at Law Hill with its 40 pupils. The same homesickness for Haworth and the moors is expressed in the poetry she wrote at Law Hill, only now her duties began at six in the morning and ended at eleven at night. Nor was Charlotte there to share her bed. When Charlotte heard of Emily's situation, she protested: "This is slavery. I fear she will never stand it." This time Emily was back in the parsonage in six months.

The experience of Law Hill carried Brontë deeper into the world of Gondal. Her social contact produced profound anxiety, while her isolation in her fantasy reduced that anxiety. It was at this point, at her return to Haworth, that she sought a new dimension. In her poetry, she speaks of the visitations which she felt endowed her with the power to create. Brontë viewed this cosmic force as inseparable from her own creativity.

In the following poem, the Visitant is speaking to her:

> . . . Thy mind is ever moving,
> In regions dark to thee;
> Recall its useless roving—
> Come back and dwell with me. . .
>
> I've watched thee every hour.
> I know my mighty sway,
> I know my magic power
> To drive thy griefs away.
> (Hatfield, 1941, pp. 163–164)

Given another context, one could construe this as a love poem between two persons. The Visitant is persuasive, seductive, masculine. Yet sometimes the voice is Brontë's as she speaks to her Visitant.

> . . . And thou art now a spirit pouring
> Thy presence into all—
> The essence of the Tempest's roaring
> And of the Tempest's fall—
>
> A universal influence
> From thine own influence free;
> A principle of life, intense,
> Lost to mortality (1941, p. 165).

Frequently, Brontë and her Visitant are in dialogue:

> . . . I sat in silent musing
> The soft wind waved my hair.
> It told me Heaven was glorious,
> And sleeping Earth was fair.

I needed not its breathing
To bring such thoughts to me
But still it whispered lowly
'How dark the woods will be!

The thick leaves in my murmur
Are rustling like a dream.
And all their myriad voices
Instinct with spirit seem.'

I said, 'Go gentle singer,
Thy wooing voice is kind,
But do not think its music
Has power to reach my mind.

Play with the scented flower,
The young tree's supple bough,
And leave my human feelings
In their own course to flow!'

The wanderer would not leave me;
Its kiss grew warmer still
'O come,' it sighed so sweetly,
'I'll win thee gainst thy will.

Have we not been from childhood friends?
Have I not loved thee long?
As long as thou hast loved the night
Whose silence makes my song.

And when thy heart is laid at rest
Beneath the churchyard stone
I shall have time enough to mourn
And thou to be alone' (1941, pp. 146-147).

Two voices, two parts of Brontë's undifferentiated self, merged into her narcissism. She made the romantic fusion between herself and her Visitant (Morrison & Morrison, 1988). Brontë was the courted Beloved, and she was also the seductive lover. Her experience indicates an internal need state that had been frustrated in its efforts to gain satisfaction. Whether she needed to relieve her anxiety or to protect herself from narcissistic injury, she sought out the Visitant as a means of making herself whole. Then, going beyond the need state and frustration, she moves to the third component of the romantic love experience: idealization. The Visitant has the power, the glory, the creativity that Brontë desires. More significantly, the Visitant is fascinated with her and tries to seduce her to his will. Here Brontë moves to the final component of the romantic love experience: fantasy. Her possession of the Visitant will satisfy all of her frustrated needs and result in an euphoric, conflict-free existence. Brontë's experience of romantic love is unique because no tangible person is involved. The Visitant is the power of Nature and creativity, but he exists as a projection of Brontë's unconscious.

This romantic fusion and Brontë's intense passion resonate in the following poem.

> . . . All through the night, your glorious eyes
> Were gazing down in mine,
> And with a full heart's thankful sighs
> I blessed that watch divine!
>
> I was at peace, and drank your beams
> As they were life to me
> And revelled in my changeful dreams
> Like petrel [sea birds] on the sea.
>
> Thought followed thought—star followed star
> Through the boundless regions on,
> While one sweet influence, near and far,
> Thrilled through and proved us one.
>
> Why did the morning rise to break
> So great, so pure a spell,
> And scorch with fire the tranquil cheek
> Where your cool radiance fell? . . .
>
> O Stars and Dreams and Gentle Night;
> O Night and Stars return!
> And hide me from the hostile light
> That does not warm, but burn . . . (1941, pp. 225-227).

It is the "hostile light" of day that "burns," that destroys her fantasy of this union. Brontë was 19 when these Visitations began. Her need for Gondal grew progressively stronger, and by the time she was 22 she wanted to live only in this world. As she was experiencing these Visitations, her Gondal heroes now engaged in love affairs. Lacking any personal experience in love, Brontë poured the power and intensity of her own romantic ideation into these fictional characters of her paracosm. It is something she will do later with Catherine and Heathcliff in *Wuthering Heights*.

According to Silvey and MacKeith (1988), most children are giving up their paracosms by age 12 or 13. It is significant that both Charlotte and Branwell wrote formal farewells to their paracosmic kingdom, Angria, in their early twenties, but Emily, who shared her writing with Anne, was actively engaged in writing about Gondal until her death at age 30. This paracosm still provided her with compensatory control, enabled her to retain her self-concept, and functioned as a focus for her creativity.

Emily Brontë's twenty-seventh birthday letter (1845) to Anne states: "The Gondals still flourish bright as ever. I am at present working on the First War" (Gérin, 1971, p. 179). She also refers to a three-day walking excursion in which she and Anne had spent much time working on the development of their Gondal characters.

But Charlotte was a powerful maternal figure for Emily, and at age 24 Emily consented to study in Brussels with Charlotte. They would prepare themselves to open a school near Haworth. After they had spent nine months in Brussels, Aunt Elizabeth Branwell died and both women returned home. Charlotte later returned to Brussels; Emily remained at home, alone with her father. She never left the parsonage again.

Besides Emily Brontë's adulation of her Visitant, her idealization of Branwell was a major force in her life. The two-year period they had shared in the parsonage without Charlotte and Anne had an enormous impact on Emily, who was 17 to 19 at that time. Branwell, the "little king," had returned from the Royal Academy in London, so overwhelmed by the competition that he had not even submitted his application to the school. Without even one interview, he fled to a London tavern where he spent the money Charlotte and his family had provided for him. All of this he had confided to Emily; for his father and aunt he invented a story of robbery. Branwell's inability to confront the world outside the parsonage paralleled Emily's own inability to leave their home. She empathized with him, identified with him, and supported him.

As Branwell shared his feelings of failure with Emily, he also expressed his defiance against a world which had defeated him. In Emily's Gondal poetry at this time the recurring themes of guilt and failure permeate her work. She never doubted that Branwell would eventually triumph over his situation. If she identified with Branwell's guilt and failure, then his victory would be hers as well. But Branwell's life became a downhill race toward self-destruction. Nothing worked for him: teaching, writing, painting, clerking, tutoring. Finally, fired as a tutor because of an alleged love affair with his patron's wife, Branwell returned to the parsonage and turned to opium and alcohol.

Psychologically and emotionally, everyone abandoned Branwell except Emily. She knew now that he would never triumph, never give her the victory she had sought in her identification with him. Yet it was Emily who carried her drunken brother upstairs to his bed; Emily who broke the family rules to unlock the door for him; Emily who dragged him from his flaming bed and quenched the fire. And all the while she raged at her family, especially Charlotte, who rejected Branwell; she raged at a world that could inflict such pain upon a beloved brother. With her habitual taciturnity, Emily said nothing, but she wrote.

Wuthering Heights began as Emily Brontë experienced Branwell's devastation. It is a rage coupled with the notion of the destructive power of love that she explores; it is the dark side of romantic love. And it begins with childhood. It is not insignificant that Brontë seems to have created an orphan world in her novel. Virtually, every child in the first generation (Heathcliff, Catherine, Hindley) and in the second (young Catherine, Hindley) loses one parent, and it is usually the mother (Fraser, 1988).

Heathcliff, an abandoned orphan, becomes the childhood companion of his foster sister, Catherine. They play together, suffer together, a union of two against the world. But when the father dies, Hindley, his natural son, takes over Wuthering Heights and separates the two children. Because of his jealousy, Hindley cruelly exiles Heathcliff from the family. Catherine watches Heathcliff deteriorate. Thinking that Catherine has abandoned him, Heathcliff runs away before he can hear that Catherine identifies with him, that his pain and humiliation are hers as well. To Nelly, the old servant, she confides: "I *am* Heathcliff—he's always, always in my mind—not as a pleasure, anymore than I am always a pleasure to myself—but as my own being . . ." (Brontë, 1960, p. 86).

The merging of the two lovers into one identity is the epitome of romantic love and ideation; it is also Brontë's expression of the fusion, a bond with her brother. The brother-sister romance of Heathcliff and Catherine who have shared their world since childhood is a reflection of Brontë's own experience. The themes of separation and abandonment are paramount here. Brontë was in the midst of watching Branwell separate himself from her, his family, and his previous life as he, too deteriorated; as the family, especially Charlotte, abandoned him, Emily felt his pain and humiliation. Yet she also felt abandoned, and with it a tremendous anger; she is furious at being left; enraged at what she is losing; terrified at the thought of separation. At one level she understood that she was losing more than Branwell, more than Charlotte; it was her own survival that hung in the balance. The powerful emotions she felt in response to her themes of separation and abandonment were poured into her lovers: Catherine and Heathcliff.

In her merging of the lovers, Brontë becomes both characters; she is Catherine responding to Heathcliff, but she is also Heathcliff, expressing herself through him. It is a translation in human terms of what Brontë experienced and wrote in her poetry about the relationship between herself and her Visitant. Once more the interchangeability of self in romantic ideation is demonstrated, but now the concept of the Beloved centers on the two human lovers. Just as Catherine identifies with Heathcliff, so he claims her as a part of himself as he cries, "I cannot live without my life! I cannot live without my soul!" (p. 177). Catherine echoes, "I love him . . . because he's more myself than I am. Whatever our souls are made of, his and mine are the same" (p. 85). Heinrich Zimmer defines this same phenomenon in the context of Lancelot and Guinevere: "Each had discovered in the other, not a devoted human companion, but the perfect counter-actor on an ideal, superhuman stage of abstract yet fatal passion. Each was related to the other, not as to a human being, but as to a discovery of a lost, required, separated portion of the soul. They were not two but one: each a projection of the unconscious of the other" (Zimmer, 1973, p. 160).

This romantic fusion is asexual; it is a passionate love affair of the soul, a continuation of the child romance relationship. The body never enters the dialogue. The *Wuthering Heights* lovers' most intense scene occurs when Catherine is almost nine months pregnant with her husband Edgar's child, but her "condition" isn't worth mentioning because it is her spirit, not her body, that Heathcliff claims. Just as Brontë sought out her Visitant to find her wholeness, so Heathcliff rages against everyone, everything, until his end, begging for Catherine's spirit to complete him. This separation from his Beloved is a separation from himself; it is this ultimate horror that he cannot endure. Catherine dies early in the novel, and once more the body is insignificant. It is Catherine's spirit that Heathcliff covets. It is Catherine's spirit that pervades the novel.

Brontë believed in spirits. Certainly, the image of her dead sister Maria crying at the parsonage window remained with her forever. And her own relationship with her Visitant convinced her of an eternal, creative cosmic force that existed within her and outside her, the romantic merging discussed previously. She believed in the indestructibility of the human soul. This concept of spirits offered an alternative to death, an experience she had witnessed numerous times, and a theme that appears frequently in her poetry. The death of Heathcliff is a triumph over death, because it will bring the romantic merging of his own soul with Catherine's. Brontë's spirits do not reflect the gentle Christian teachings of her church. Rather, they symbolize power and total freedom. The spirit of Catherine punishes Heathcliff by wantonly showing herself to a stranger, Lockwood, while never permitting Heathcliff to see her. It is a narcissistic, childlike act.

Besides the asexuality of Heathcliff and Catherine, one sees numerous examples of childlike behavior: their narcissistic desire to please only themselves, their disregard for social convention. Aconventional, amoral, they exist solely for themselves. Egocentric, they believe the world was created for them. Even Edgar's response to his wife's attentions to Heathcliff demonstrates this behavior, as he upbraids her: "It is impossible for you to be *my* friend, and *his* at the same time" (p. 124). It is also commensurate with Brontë's level of sexual experience. And while she understood social conventions, in the characters of Nelly and Lockwood, it is Catherine and Heathcliff who slap the face of society with their narcissistic behavior. Heathcliff, especially, becomes the chronic, raging child.

Heathcliff's passion was born from Brontë's own frustration and rage. He is a brutal man who uses his power to tyrannize all who have the misfortune to cross his path. Even Catherine, who knows him best, tells Isabelle, "He is a pitiless, wolfish man" (p. 108). He snarls; he howls; he smashes his head against a tree at Catherine's funeral, leaving blood on the bark. No one touches him emotionally because his egocentric rage embraces his world. And he rages against the separation from Catherine which destroys his wholeness.

When Brontë finished *Wuthering Heights,* she still believed that the creative power she shared with her Visitant was eternal. Her paracosm of Gondal was intact. The compensatory mechanisms of her fantasy still protected her. Then things changed very quickly.

Wuthering Heights was published in December, 1847. For two years Brontë had watched the gradual decline of Branwell, the animosity between him and his family, his exclusion from the girls' publishing ventures, the destruction of his mind and body. Branwell was approaching death and everyone knew it. As a child, Emily had experienced the deaths of her mother and her two older sisters. The paracosm of Glasstown, shared with her siblings, provided her with a compensatory mode that extended throughout her life. But now she confronted death as an adult, the death of a sibling with whom she identified. Part of Emily was dying with Branwell.

In 1848 Emily Brontë stopped writing. Her Visitant had abandoned her, and thus her creative powers deserted her too. She now doubted the immortality of the soul. Earlier, in 1844, she had written:

> . . . And am I wrong to worship where
> Faith cannot doubt nor Hope despair
> Since my own soul can grant my prayer?
> Speak, God of visions, plead for me
> And tell why I have chosen thee! (Brontë, 1941, pp. 208-209).

Now, four years later, the romantic fusion between Brontë and her Visitant ended. She was alone. Branwell died on September 24, 1848.

After the funeral service for Branwell in October, Emily Brontë never left the inside of the parsonage again. Giving up the moors and her love of nature was a self-imposed death sentence (Fraser, 1988). Barely a month after Branwell's death she did not even answer when spoken to. She was in deep depression. Anne, coughing and diagnosed with tuberculosis, was deemed incurable, but Emily moved more rapidly. Within a week of Branwell's funeral, Emily was ill. She refused to see a physician, to take medication, or even to rest. She insisted on doing all her chores. She would not accept help or advice from anyone, and she refused to speak to Charlotte about her feelings. Each day she retreated more into herself. Her inflamed lungs surrendered to tuberculosis, but they were assisted by a depressed spirit, just as her mind had betrayed her body at Roe Head. On December 19, 1848, less than three months after Branwell's death, Emily Brontë died; she was 30 years old.

Five months later, Anne, 29, followed Emily in death. Charlotte survived for six more years. The intense regrouping of the Brontë siblings after the deaths of their mother and sisters had permitted them to explore a rich, creative dimension of themselves in shared paracosms that influenced their entire lives.

For Emily Brontë, the early loss was traumatic to her developing identity and sense of self. The trauma of the early loss of her mother when she was three and the subsequent loss of her sisters when she was six played a critical role in developing her sense of self and identity. Her diffusion and fragility persisted her whole life, manifesting in her asocial behavior and the creation of compensatory paracosms. Both rage at and identification with the lost object of love are early and constant themes in Brontë's creative works. Unlike Barrie, Kerouac, or Dinesen, she did not identify with or take on characteristics of the dead loved ones. She could not consciously explore her feminine nature; counter-phobically, she reacted against it. Brontë's identification was with her idealized image of Branwell, and by challenging the moors and their storms and exploring the destructive forces of Nature, she transformed their terror and her anger into something knowable and nurturing. This conflicted internal image, both frightening and creative, resolved itself with the romantically idealized Visitant. He was Brontë's attempt to reduce her anxiety generated by a fragmented sense of self and her rage at the loss of love through death. Brontë created the Visitant as a means of making herself whole. With the demise of Branwell, her fragile masculine identification deteriorated, and the Visitant abandoned her. But not before her experience of the merging of self and loss of self in a cosmos of wild emotions evolved creatively into her poetry and into her novel, *Wuthering Heights*.

CHAPTER 7

J. M. Barrie: A Search for the Eternal Boy of Neverland

"I want always to be a little boy and to have fun!"
Peter Pan
J. M. Barrie (1860-1937)

The epitome of childhood loss, romantic ideation, and subsequent creativity is seen in J. (James) M. Barrie, the creator of Peter Pan. Peter Pan is the eternal boy. In the context of Neverland, he shall never grow up; his life will be one fun-filled adventure, for he shall play forever. This idealized state of perpetual childhood and Peter, the unique boy who enjoys it, represent the romantic ideation of their creator. Ironically, it was the death of Barrie's brother, David, that gave birth to these imaginative creations—35 years later.

On the eve of David's fourteenth birthday, in January, 1867, he was killed in a skating accident. He had lent his skates to a friend ,who then lost control as he sped across the ice, smashing into David, who fell heavily, head first, onto the ice. His skull was fractured; he never regained consciousness and survived only a few hours. It was an enormous shock to the family, especially to his mother, Margaret Ogilvy (who had retained her maiden name in accordance with an old Scots custom), for David had been her favorite.

David was tall, athletic, handsome, charming, and emulating the academic achievements of the oldest of the three brothers, Alexander, who had been a scholar at Aberdeen University and then opened a private school. At this time, James was six years old; small, the runt of the family, he lacked the physical appearance and academic promise of David. Even before the accident, James lived in the shadow of this brother: one boy had been so special, the other so ordinary. As a child, Barrie never knew David. He recalls, "I remember very little about him, only that he was a merry-faced boy who ran like a squirrel up a tree and shook the cherries into my lap." He also remembered playing with his younger sister, Maggie, under the table on which rested David's coffin. Death locked David into eternal boyhood. Never would Barrie have the opportunity to know this idealized brother who would never grow up, could never grow up; thus the state of eternal boyhood itself became an ideal. As a boy, Barrie sought to emulate the live David; as an adult, he would seek the dead David in his ideal state. The image of David, the eternal boy, would haunt J. M. Barrie for 71 more years. He would become inextricably bound to this ephemeral shadow, which would become such a vital part of himself.

With the death of his brother David, Barrie experienced a concomitant loss of his mother, Margaret Ogilvy. Overwhelmed by her loss, she "was always delicate from that hour, and for many months she was very ill." In her darkened room, she lay in bed with the family christening robe beside her, constantly crying, oblivious to the needs of her family. Barrie writes, "I peeped in many times at the door and then went to the stair and sat on it and sobbed." It was his sister, Jane Ann, who found the solitary boy on the stairs. She was 20 years old and had assumed her mother's responsibilities after David's death. She urged James to go to their mother and tell her that she had another boy. It was a crucial event.

> The room was dark, and when I heard the door shut and no sound came from the bed I was afraid, and I stood still. I suppose I was breathing hard, or perhaps was crying, for after a time I heard a listless voice that had never been listless before say "Is that you?" I think the tone hurt me, for I made no answer, and then the voice said more anxiously, "Is that you?" again. I thought it was the dead boy she was speaking to, and I said in a little lonely voice, "No, it's no him, it's just me." Then I heard a cry, and my mother turned in bed and though it was dark I knew that she was holding out her arms (Barrie, 1901, p. 232).

From that moment Barrie became obsessed with making his mother forget the dead David and focus on the living James. Barrie writes that he had "an intense desire to become so like him [David] that even my mother should not see the difference." She told him that she always loved David's cheery whistle, how it brightened her at work to hear him; she even described how David stood with his legs apart and his hands in his pockets. From David's comrades, Barrie learned how to whistle like his brother; he wore David's clothes. On one occasion he secretly put on these clothes and slipped into his mother's room: "Listen, [he] cried and began to whistle" (p. 234).

The young James became a self-appointed "physician" to his mother, spending a great deal of time with her, sitting on her bed, and attempting to make her laugh. He kept a record of these laughs with strokes on paper and proudly showed it to the family doctor each morning. Margaret Ogilvy improved. Jane Ann had told her little brother to get their mother to talk about the dead boy. As the mother recalled fond memories of David, Barrie at first became very jealous, but soon he had a model, one that would last for a life time. He was not cognizant of what "David" really meant to him, how David permeated his life, both in his childhood and in his maturity. As a young boy, Barrie idealized

David, tried to become David. This is a viable part of his identification. Since he never knew his brother, it was his mother's fantasy of David that he sought. This compensatory wish to become his brother resulted in an identification transforming the dead David into the living James. A part of himself that was vaguely understood by preoperational thought was lost to Barrie. What evolved was the self, based on a wish for his mother's love. Neither "self" could be adequately explored; this created an anxiety that placed Barrie "Betwixt-and-Between."

Magical thinking, another component of preoperational thought, is seen in Barrie's response to the name "David." His fusion of word and person (object) is powerful. For the rest of Barrie's life, the name "David" would surface in his art: the symbol of the ideal boy. George Davies becomes David in *The Little White Bird;* Barrie's last drama is entitled *The Boy David.*

Because the emulated, dead David is a boy, the eternal state of boyhood becomes powerful and magical as well. While Barrie remained a boy, the identification with his dead brother functioned fairly well, but as Barrie moved into his manhood, he found this situation to be impossible.

Meanwhile, as a boy, Barrie listened not only to his mother's fantasies about David, but to her memories of her own childhood. The death of her son brought memories of her mother's death. When she was eight years old, Margaret Ogilvy became the "little mother" of the house, the child-mother, caring for her father and little five-year-old brother. She shared innumerable stories about her life in Kirriemuir with the young James, and always, she was at the center: the image of a little girl-mother, wearing a magenta frock and a white pinafore, who carried her father's supper in a flagon to the distant places in Scotland where he worked as a stonecutter. Margaret Ogilvy recovered from her depression, but the stories continued. So did the intimacy between mother and son.

The Kirriemuir tales forged a bond between them, a reciprocal paracosm where they shared the power of their imagination. Soon, his mother's tales became Barrie's stories. They were so entwined that even he was not sure how it began: "On a day I conceived a glorious idea, or was it put into my head by my mother . . . the notion was nothing short of this, why should I not write the tales myself?" (Barrie, 1901, p. 254) He did write them, up in the garret of their house, and ran down the stairs to read each completed short chapter to the waiting Margaret Ogilvy. Not only was she a part of the creative process of writing, but she would later provide the content and the substance of characterization for Barrie. It was her stories that would become his stories.

These stories about life in Kirriemuir, *Auld Licht Idylls* (1901), are told not only from Margaret Ogilvy's perspective, but from her experiences as a child 60 years earlier. Barrie was 28 years old when he wrote these tales, and the center of his creative vision was the little girl-mother whom he idealized and adored. Later, in *Margaret Ogilvy* (1901), written as a tribute to his mother after her death, Barrie, aged 36, writes: "I soon grew tired of writing tales, unless I see a little girl, of whom my mother has told me, wandering confidently through the pages. Such a grasp as her memory of her girlhood had upon me since I was a boy of six." Even more succinctly, he writes:

> I suppose, mother, it was because you were most at home in your town, and there was never much pleasure to me in writing of people who could not have known you, nor of squares or winds you never passed through, nor the country-side where you never carried your father's dinner in a flagon. There is scarce a house in all my books where I have not seemed to see you a thousand times, bending over the fireplace and winding up the clock . . . the little girl in my story wears a magenta frock and white pinafore (Barrie, 1901, pp. 335-336).

This paracosmic bond exists until his mother's death. As an adult, Barrie corresponded daily with his mother. She carefully preserved the hundreds of letters from him, always sleeping with the latest one beneath her sheet; Barrie's last letter was found there when she died. And after her death this creative, paracosmic process would be repeated with the Davies boys, first with George, and then with Michael. It is another search, another quest for the self that Barrie romanticized: his mother's fantasy of his brother David as a boy. Neither time nor age would alter the vivid image of the child-mother who lived in the richness of Barrie's imagination. Even Margaret Ogilvy's laughter remained in her son's memory as that of a "merry child," eternally ageless; she was his ideal, sent by God "to open the minds of all who looked to beautiful thoughts" (p. 227).

While Margaret Ogilvy would never read the words her son wrote in tribute to her, she knew her power over him, and she delighted in being the focal point for his writing. Barrie records a conversation between his mother and Jane Ann as Margaret Ogilvy tells her daughter, "He tries to keep me out [of his writing] but he canna—it's more than he can do!" (p. 328). When mother and son discuss the need of a writer to know both man and woman, she chides the young Barrie, "I'm the only woman you know well." He replies, "Then I must make you my heroine." And so he did.

Because the romantic ideation between mother and son was reciprocal, it became more powerful and credulous for both of them. While he became the eternal boy who would never grow up, she became the little girl-mother from her lost childhood. Later, they would share the paracosm of Neverland: he would become Peter Pan, the boy who refuses to grow up, and she would become Wendy, the child-mother.

Barrie was not fatherless. David Barrie supported his large family as a weaver. A large, strong, quiet man, he never shared an intimacy with his son; nor is he mentioned in Barrie's autobiographical writings beyond a cursory "a man I am very proud to call my father." James Barrie's intimacy was exclusively with Margaret Ogilvy.

It is not surprising that Barrie was reluctant to give up this intimacy of his childhood. Besides the stories he wrote, he created little theatricals and performed them in Margaret Ogilvy's washhouse, a prototype for the house he would later create for Wendy. It was a creative and fruitful period for the young boy until he reached age 12. Then he entered a school where sports were more important than stories about a little girl carrying her father's supper in a flagon. As Barrie later said, "nothing that happens after we are 12 matters very much." Already, there is nostalgia for the past, a fear of the future.

Barrie confides, "the horror of my boyhood was that I knew a time would come when I must also give up the games, and how it was to be done, I saw not. . . . I felt that I must continue playing in secret." Yet a compensation for Barrie then, as earlier in his childhood, was writing; so it would always be. During his five years at Dumfries Academy he wrote his first play, *Bandelaro the Bandit,* for the school's drama club and found a friend, Stuart Gordon, with whom he could share his make-believe work.

But now Barrie's boyhood was indeed leaving him. At age 17, entering adolescence, he was barely five feet tall and had stopped growing. He was becoming a man but was still the size of a boy. "Being small enough to travel half ticket by rail" was a great embarrassment to him. His lack of height disturbed him enormously, and he was not successful in his relations with young women. Reluctantly, he consented to attend the University of Edinburgh; it was not his idea. Margaret Ogilvy convinced him that had his dead brother, David, lived, *he* would have gone to the university. Barrie had no choice.

Entering manhood was painful for Barrie; he was miserable. Desolate at Edinburgh, he became taciturn and diffident. It was one of the loneliest times of his life. He wrote about himself in his notebook at this time: "he is very young looking; the trial of his life is that he is always thought a boy" (Barrie, 1901, p. 12).

> Far finer and nobler things in the world than loving a girl and getting her.
> Grow up and have to give up marbles, awful thought.
> Greatest horror: dream I am married, wake up shrieking (Birkin, 1979, p. 12).

Just 21 years old, Barrie was already looking back at what he felt he had lost, what he could never regain. The future held little charm for him, and so to maintain a semblance of the ideal state he withdrew into himself. As he entered adulthood, it seemed natural that he would relate these present experiences to earlier, richer times; that he would seek to recapture the magic that he and Margaret Ogilvy had shared: the golden time of ideal images formulated through mutual romantic ideation. For Barrie, there was a supreme value in remaining a child, yet there was also great pain for a boy who remained "Betwixt-and-Between" in an adult body in an adult world. Following his time at the university, Barrie worked as a journalist for the Nottingham Journal (1882-1884). He was unsuccessful and unemployed after two years, and it was the *Auld Licht Idylls* stories from Margaret Ogilvy that began his writing career. Numerous articles on the Auld Licht community led to its publication. *Auld Licht Idylls* (1901) and a *Window in Thrums* (1901) are novels about life in Kirriemuir, as is *The Little Minister* (1901). Barrie's continued interest in the theatre eventually led to his work as a playwright. And his notebook entries during this time reflect his difficulties with women and his nightmares of marriage.

Ten years later, Barrie's nightmare of marriage emerged in an article entitled "My Ghastly Dream." He writes: "Always I see myself being married and then I wake up with the scream of a lost soul, clammy and shivering." Yet he was physically attracted to young women, especially pretty actresses whom he met in the theatre while his plays were being produced; he flirted with them. It was a delicious game, until Barrie met Mary Ansell.

Mary Ansell was lovely, petite, and soon very much in love with Barrie, who adored escorting her everywhere and watching heads turn for a second glimpse of the superb-looking young woman. Two years later, at age 34, Barrie married Ansell. It had the potential of being a perfect union. Yet two days before his wedding, Barrie wrote in his notebook:

> Our love has brought me nothing but misery.
> Boy all nerves. You are very ignorant.
> How? Must we instruct you in the mysteries of lovemaking? (Birkin, 1979, p. 29).

Barrie's words were prophetic. That the Barries' marriage had never been sexually consummated was revealed years later by Mary Barrie during their divorce proceedings. Barrie's notes had revealed the humiliation that would torture him. He turned to his writing, but notebooks were not enough. He tried to work through the complexities of his problems in a novel, *Tommy and Grizel* (Barrie, 1943).

Like his creator, Tommy agonizes over his marriage to Grizel. They were childhood friends, and now Grizel is a woman with mature feelings and emotions while Tommy is still a boy and cannot satisfy her female passions, desperately though he tries. Barrie describes their plight:

> He told her all that love meant to him and it meant everything that he thought Grizel would like it to mean. They had a honeymoon by the sea. . . . Tommy, trying to become a lover by taking thought, and Grizel, not letting on that it could not be done in that way. . . . He was a boy only. . . . And boys cannot love. Oh, is it not cruel to ask a boy to love? . . . He was a boy who could not grow up. He gave her all his affection but his passion, like an outlaw, had ever to hunt alone (Birkin, 1979, p. 40).

In working through his fictional character Tommy, Barrie was attempting to understand himself. About Tommy: "he was so fond of being a boy he could not grow up." As Barrie creatively approached this problem of being "Betwixt-and-Between" in the character of Tommy, his empathy for his creation is paramount. It is the context, not Tommy, that is at fault. "In a younger world, where there were only boys and girls, he [Tommy] might have been a gallant figure." The apology turns to open admiration: "Oh, who by striving could make himself a boy again as Tommy could! I tell you he was always irresistible then. What is genius? It is the power to be a boy again at will." While Barrie's empathy resides with Tommy, Tommy as a young adult cannot cope with reality and meets a tragic end. Ironically, it is the death of Tommy that will give birth to Peter Pan. The same problem of Betwixt-and-Between—Barrie would wrestle with it forever—he approaches from a child's perspective. He creates an eternal state of childhood that is desirable and a creature, "a gallant figure," who is enviable: Peter Pan.

Unlike Tommy, Peter Pan does not have a mature male body, nor does he function in an adult world: therein lies his strength. Indeed, he refuses to grow up. He is not confused about his values or his priorities, and he distrusts adults. Peter, who first appears in *The Little White Bird,* escaped the fate of humanity when he was seven days old: he flew out of the nursery window and back to Kensington Gardens; yet mortality had stamped him, and once there he temporarily lost his power to fly. He is neither a boy nor a bird. Old Solomon Caw, the birds' potentate, christens him: "You will be a Betwixt-and-Between." And so he is, for Barrie has given his old problem a new metaphor. The tension of two worlds and the male's vacillation between those two worlds still exist.

What saves Peter Pan from Tommy's tragic ending is the context: though he sometimes stays in the gardens, Peter's new province is Neverland. Embittered by the betrayal of adult mothers, yet yearning for maternal love, Peter, in *Peter Pan and Wendy* (Barrie, 1911), chooses a new mother. It is a little girl-mother, the young child Wendy who shall be the "mother of us all"; one can visualize her with a magenta frock and a white pinafore. The idealized images of Barrie's dead brother, David, the eternal boy, and of his mother, the little Margaret Ogilvy, provide the themes which permeated Barrie's life and pervade his creation of *Peter Pan:* the desire to emulate David and remain a boy forever in the Neverland of childhood and the possession of the little girl-mother. An essential part of Barrie's journey was to explore these themes, because they provided a key to his own identity. It was a desire to return to the ideal state, to embrace the family romance forever, and to find a unity within himself with the magic of preoperational thought. Like the name "David," the concept of Peter Pan functions as a transitional object, a metaphor for the unknown self.

The desire for eternal boyhood in the Neverland of childhood is succinctly stated by Peter, as he explains to Wendy's mother: "'I don't want ever to be a man. . . . I want always to be a little boy and have fun.' He is passionate on the issue: 'Oh Wendy's mother, if I was to wake up and feel there was a beard!'" (Barrie, 1911, p. 42).

"The most entrancing thing about him [Peter]," says Barrie, "was that he had all his first teeth . . . and his first laugh still" (pp. 16, 44), a sure sign of eternal boyhood. Clearly, physical growth is a negative step. Even in play, Peter gets anxious when Wendy pretends that he is the father of the lost boys, as she is their mother. Seeking her reassurance, he asks, "It is only make-believe, isn't it, that I am their father?" Sensing her annoyance, he apologizes, "You see . . . it would make me seem so old to be their real father." And when Wendy, in exasperation, asks what Peter's feelings for her are, he replies: "Those of a devoted son, Wendy." The sexual titillation and nuances are there, but the tragedy of Tommy and Grizel takes on a light comic tone with Peter and Wendy: as a boy, Peter has responded appropriately, and it is inconceivable that, sexually, anymore might be expected from him. Surely, Wendy, as a child, does not possess Grizel's need for sexual passion, but Wendy, too, is fated to mature.

Wendy knows, in the first paragraph of *Peter Pan,* that "[age] two is the beginning of the end"; she must grow up. Unlike Peter, she has no choice—unless she remains in Neverland. Her ultimate rejection of Neverland is her betrayal of Peter: she grows to be a mature woman with a daughter of her own. Ironically, it is the reversal of the betrayal between Tommy and Grizel, but the focal point is the male who can't or won't mature, while the female can't or won't stop growing. Even in Neverland tension exists for the character caught up in two worlds: Betwixt-and-Between. Barrie says of Wendy's maturity: "You need not be sorry for her. She was one of the kind that likes to grow up." Yet when Peter later visits Wendy, she is embarrassed that she is an adult and feels "something inside of her crying 'Woman, woman let go of me.'" The pull of the two worlds splits Peter and Wendy, just as it did Tommy and Grizel.

Here the two major themes merge as Peter sees Wendy as an adult; he is horrified that she has broken her promise to remain the little girl-mother. Peter sobs at Wendy's betrayal, at the loss of the mother whom he had come to take back to Neverland, and Wendy cannot comfort him, for "she was only a woman now," and she leaves the room. They are separated by their choices: Peter Pan will never grow up and will always remain in Neverland, while Wendy, a woman with a young daughter, must face her mortality in the real world. Peter's crying wakes Wendy's daughter, Jane. It is a reenactment of the first meeting between Wendy and Peter. When Wendy returns, Peter looks at Jane and tells Wendy "She is my mother." Wendy sighs as Jane and Peter fly off to Neverland to do the "spring-cleaning." It is the compromise between Wendy and Peter. Someday, as Wendy's hair turns white, it will be Jane's daughter, Margaret, who will fly to Neverland for Peter's spring-cleaning. Each generation of daughters will be Peter's "mother" in turn, and thus it will go on, says Barrie, "so long as children are gay and innocent and heartless."

Peter Pan will remain the eternal boy; it is someone else who fathers the daughters, who in turn become Peter's little girl-mothers. It is a perfect solution, for Peter possesses the desired female object and does not have to confront "growing up," which means male maturity and sexual function.

Eleven years later, Barrie wrote in his notebooks, "It is as if long after writing *Peter Pan* its true meaning came to me—desperate attempt to grow up but can't."

Six years after this entry, which is in 1928, in the revised stage directions for the drama *Peter Pan,* when Peter states he wants always to be a little boy, to have fun, Barrie added in parentheses "so perhaps he thinks, but it is only his greatest pretend" (Birkin, 1979). No one knows how conscious Barrie was of the character of Peter Pan when he first created him, but surely his notes indicate an increased awareness of Peter's relevance to himself. Barrie's explorations of the themes that Peter and Wendy pursue are creative attempts to come to self-knowledge through magical cognition—where children can fly and never grow up. Barrie's identification with Peter is explicit, but implicit is his identification with Wendy. She is more than the idealized girlhood image of Margaret Ogilvy; she is a viable part of Barrie himself.

This maternal part of Barrie is seen in *The Little White Bird,* and the little boy who inspired these feelings and the subsequent book was George Llewelyn Davies. Wearing a bright red velvet tam-o-shanter, George was a beautiful five-year-old boy when Barrie, then 37, noticed him in Kensington Gardens as Barrie took his St. Bernard, Porthos, on daily walks. There were three Davies boys; George had two brothers: Jack was four and Peter was still in his pram, but it was George who captured Barrie's affection and soon started to dominate his life.

The Davies family soon became the most significant people in Barrie's life. Margaret Ogilvy had been dead for two years when he met them. It all started with George. To amuse and to entertain the little boy, Barrie invented the story of Peter Pan as they walked alone together in Kensington Gardens. To engage him, Barrie would wiggle his ears and perform magic feats with his eyebrows; not only could he tell George about fairies, but he could read fairy writing. Little George was completely seduced.

At a narcissistic level, their relationship was reciprocal, for Barrie was captivated by the beautiful little boy. His notebooks are filled with the things George said, experiences they shared, and George's reactions to them:

- The queer pleasure it gives when George tells me to lace his shoes.
- George burying face not to show crying.
- Little White Bird book described to me by George.
- L.W.B. Telling George what love is . . . in answer to George's inquires, about how to write a story (Birkin, 1979, p. 56).

In Barrie's notes he reveals that George, thinly disguised, becomes "David" when Barrie writes *The Little White Bird* (1902). The choice of name is significant, because George is transformed to the romantic object of ideation, the symbol of Barrie's dead, idealized brother. Yet George became something much more for Barrie: the son Barrie never fathered. In *The Little White Bird,* Barrie, assuming the person of the old Captain, writes about David: "He addresses me as father when he is in a hurry only, and never have I dared to ask him to use the name. He says, 'Come, father,' with an accursed beautiful carelessness. So let it be, David, for a little while longer. I like to hear him say it in front of others, as in shops . . . the shopkeepers accept me as his father, and I cannot explain the particular pleasure this gives me."

Barrie loved the notion of being a father, because it legitimized a mature sexuality and a capacity for responsibility that he didn't possess. It corroborated his physical success as a male. And, of course, the child he "fathered" was beautiful, intelligent, and spirited: a further indication of his superior genes and a superb transitional object for his idealized dead brother.

The old Captain, the narrator in *The Little White Bird* who courts the little David, is a gentle, lonely bachelor who pretends that he also has a son, whose name is Timothy. This creature of his imagination is described in sentimental and nostalgic terms; the poignancy of the longing for this son's reality permeates the narrative, but the old Captain surrenders his fantasy of Timothy for the live David. His role as a parent is still paramount for him. While he thrills to the child calling him "father," it is a maternal aspect of the old man that is blatantly displayed. Not only does the Captain compete with David's nurse and mother for David's affection, but he states, "David and I had a tremendous adventure. It was thus, he passed the night with me." The chapter is appropriately called "An Interloper."

The point of the adventure, says the Captain, is to do all the things for David precisely as they are done for him each evening at his own home. While he puzzles how this could possibly be an adventure for David, he reveals his own feelings: "But I have now said enough to show you what an adventure it was to me." He covertly swallows a brandy as he draws a hot bath for the child, who "slipped from my arms like a trout." At David's bedtime they find a new little bed placed close to the larger one, and next to it is David's treat of milk and biscuit—with a chocolate on the top. The delicacy of the preparations for the little boy and the sensitivity to his needs are both here. As the Captain undresses the child, it is the intimacy between them that affects the old bachelor profoundly. The child's naturalness in accepting these intimate acts from his hands, the perfect sense of trust between them, thrills the Captain. He undresses David down to his "little braces" and then says, "I cannot proceed in public with the disrobing of David." Yet the ultimate is holding this child in his bed all night—for David was frightened to sleep alone. While David thrashes all over the bed and all over the Captain, "he always retained possession of my finger." It is the Captain who lies awake reliving every beautiful detail of their time together that evening: it is the affect of a lover. In loving the boy David, the old Captain can love himself as a boy. The identities of George and David and of Barrie as the old Captain are transparent. The old Captain also demonstrates the reflections of a delicate father or perhaps, more precisely, of a mother with her son.

Barrie's identity was very complex. "Betwixt-and-Between" meant more than his vacillation between man and boy and his strong identity with the dead boy David. The paracosm he shared with Margaret Ogilvy also touched his sense of self: he romanticized the beautiful, perfect child-mother who was eternally youthful. It was George Llewelyn Davies who gave Barrie the opportunity to experience the richness of a maternal role and to explore another dimension of himself: first with George as a young boy in *The Little White Bird,* and later with George as a young man. It was George's mother, Sylvia, who furthered that journey.

Like her son, Sylvia, too, is thinly disguised in *The Little White Bird.* She is David's mother, with whom the old Captain is competing for the little boy's affection. However, while the old bachelor is overtly hostile to her, the real Sylvia was courted by J. M. Barrie. She was as physically beautiful as her sons, to whom she was devoted; for Barrie she became the romantic ideation of motherhood, just as her boys, especially George, embodied the ideal tenets of boyhood. When Barrie discovered this gorgeous family, he was determined to make them his own. He took innumerable photographs of them; some are of Sylvia alone, but many of them show her with her sons (there were no daughters). While some are obviously posed, others are candid and show the mother and sons in various stages of undress at the beach; again those intimate maternal scenes are portrayed. But Barrie wanted more than pictures.

To make Sylvia his own "mother," he renamed her. Because everyone else called her Sylvia, he chose to call her Jocelyn, her middle name, in his many letters to her. He sent her presents, theatre tickets; offered her excursions, dinners, and diversions of all kinds. He flirted with her outrageously, safe in the knowledge that she adored her barrister-husband, Arthur, who was as handsome as his wife, and that sexually Barrie would never be tested. How deliciously titillating; how close to Neverland. The beautiful Sylvia without her boys could not have charmed Barrie; it was the combination of mother and sons that drew him and captivated him. The only objects courted as furiously as Sylvia herself were her sons. Barrie was financially successful with his plays, and he was generous with his money. George and his brothers were inundated with gifts and toys; treated to the theatre and ice cream-cakes; they loved it, and clearly Barrie reveled in their company: for they gave him something else.

As Barrie explored these facets of himself in the context of the boys, he gained from them the inspiration and the impetus for creativity. They functioned as his muses. Again, it had started with George. Peter Pan had been the topic of endless discussions between them. In *The Little White Bird,* Barrie (1902) records the creative process:

> [This] is our way with a story: First I tell it to him [David], and then he tells it to me, the understanding being that it is quite a different story; and then I retell it with his additions, and so we go on until no one could say whether it is more his story or mine. In this story of Peter Pan, for instance, the bold narrative and most of the moral reflections are mine, though not all, for this boy can be a stern moralist; but the interesting bits about the ways and customs of babies in the bird-stage are mostly reminiscences of [his], recalled by pressing his hands to his temples and thinking hard (p. 158).

It is a child's perception that describes the beautiful Serpentine Lake in Kensington Gardens. Whether George pressed his head and "remembered" or Barrie recorded the boy's observations, it is significant that this description of Barrie's utilizes the magical approach to experience that young children still employ. Barrie writes, "It is a lovely lake and there is a drowned forest at the bottom of it. If you peer over the edge you can see the trees all growing upside down, and they say that at night there are also drowned stars in it." Or as they stroll together in the Broad Walk, "David wondered if it began little, and grew and grew, until it was quite grown up and whether the other [smaller] walks are its babies."

Barrie replicates the creative process of sharing his paracosm with Margaret Ogilvy. Now he and George create and share the world of Peter Pan. It is an extensive paracosm. Barrie not only valued George's preoperational cognition, his magical thinking, but understood and participated in it. With George, and later his brothers, Barrie would explore the creative richness of his imagination.

Play and the creative process merged for Barrie in the summer of 1901: it would be the finest summer in his life. Years prior to his divorce, he and his wife, Mary, spent the summer at Black Lake Cottage, a five-minute walk from Tilford Cottage where the Davies family were vacationing. For the entire month of August, Barrie and "his boys" were inseparable; the long summer days were filled with play. The lake became a South Seas Lagoon; the boys were pirates and Indians; even Porthos, the St. Bernard, wore the papier-mâché mask of a lion. Each day they shared their wonderful adventures. Barrie, inventing the script spontaneously, used his favorite book as a boy, *The Coral Island,* as the basis for their escapades. He would pause to photograph the boys or to jot down ideas. He became the pirate Captain Swarthy, a dark, sinister figure who frequently forced the boys to walk the plank into the shallow waters of Black Lake. That Sylvia and Arthur had to interfere when the use of real arrows and long-bladed knives was interjected says something about Barrie's own absorption in the play. He was in his element and enormously happy as he engaged with the boys, now aged eight, seven, and four, in their games. What hidden knowledge did Barrie find in that special world they had created that summer with the richness of their imagination? Surely, Captain Swarthy became Captain Hook, and the boys, collectively, merged into Peter Pan, but that would come later. Barrie took the photographs and used them as 35 illustrations for a book to commemorate that summer. Bound in cloth, it was entitled "*The Boy Castaways of Black Lake Island*—being a record of the terrible adventures of the Brothers Davies in the summer of 1901 faithfully set forth by Peter Llewelyn Davies." It was published by Barrie himself. How personal the experience was is indicated by the fact that Barrie did not want this to be a commercial venture; he printed two copies of this book—one of which he gave to Arthur Davies, who promptly lost it, leaving it in a railway carriage.

That this summer was the creative genesis of Peter Pan is clearly documented in Barrie's notebooks. It is also another indication of how the interplay between himself and the Davies family or the family romance formulated a basis for his creativity. When he met George, Barrie was working on *Tommy and Grizel* and making notes, though he didn't know it at the time, for *The Little White Bird*. It is not coincidental that Tommy's failure to mature as a sexual male is transformed into the glory of the male who can't grow up, because concomitant with the little boy is the special knowledge he has of the world, the mythic, magical approach to experience that transforms it and makes it transcend reality. It is a world that is open exclusively to children. Later, in 1928, Barrie acknowledged his creative debt: "I suppose I always knew that I made Peter by rubbing the five of you [there were eventually five Davies boys] violently together, as savages with two sticks produce a flame. I am sometimes asked who and what Peter is, but that is all he is, the spark I got from you." George and his brothers became Barrie's muses as well as "play fellows." They animated him, took him out of one of his frequent bouts of depression, inspired him. Wendy, however, was not yet created, and while Margaret Ogilvy and Barrie himself formulate a part of her, there is the explicit part played by Sylvia Jocelyn Davies.

When Sylvia's fourth boy, Michael, was born in 1900, Barrie acted as if this child was her first-born son. Indeed it was for Barrie, since the other boys had existed when he first met the Davies family. While George was clearly his established favorite among the boys, Michael might have been the imaginary Timothy of the old Captain in *The Little White Bird* for Barrie, because he was immediately drawn to this child, who later became very special to him. Michael, more than any of his brothers, looked like Sylvia. Sensitive, intelligent, physically gorgeous, Michael represented those ideal qualities of boyhood as well as those aspects of his mother that Barrie adored. Always, to Barrie, Sylvia would be the handsome mother of a family of beautiful boys, the eternal object of Barrie's romantic fantasy. Surely, she was his mother, too, as he "played" with her sons. In *Peter Pan in Kensington Gardens* (1901), Peter rapturously says to his girl friend: "O Maimie . . . do you know why I love you? It is because you are like a beautiful nest." The metaphor is appropriate for Sylvia.

While the possession of the Davies family had provided a basis for Barrie's creativity, the loss of that relationship also affected Barrie and his journey to himself. Abruptly, without warning, Arthur Llewelyn Davies was diagnosed with cancer of the jaw. As a strong masculine presence in the family, Arthur had tolerated Barrie's intrusion into his home and indulged his wife's taste for luxury by permitting her to accept Barrie's gifts and favors, which Arthur could not provide himself; Barrie's wealth far superceded the income of the Davies family. In 1907, Arthur Davies died; it was an incalculable loss to the family. After Arthur's death, Barrie was magnanimous in his generosity to Sylvia and "his boys."

The second tragic loss was the death of Sylvia three years later (1910) from the same disease: cancer. The "beautiful nest" was gone, and Barrie himself would try to provide it. The families of Arthur and Sylvia could not financially handle all five boys (one more boy, Nico, had followed Michael's birth); yet no one wanted to separate the brothers, and Barrie had insisted on becoming their guardian. Generous, kind, sensitive, and well-meaning, Barrie's attempt at fatherhood was a tragic failure. He could play with his boys; he could be one of them, but discipline, authority, and structure were not in his repertoire. He would indulge them shamelessly, such as renting a manor house on a Scottish island and later an island itself for their summer holiday. They went to the best schools; ate in the finest restaurants; enjoyed every material pleasure that Barrie could give them: clothes, toys, amusements, and holidays. It was not enough. Ironically, the two Davies boys whom Barrie loved the most and who had provided him with creative inspiration were the ones he would lose: George and Michael.

In 1915, four and a half years after Sylvia's death, George Llewelyn Davies was killed in World War I in France. During the war, the one book he had taken with him into the trenches was *The Little White Bird: his* book; the love song that Barrie had written for him; the beautiful fantastic paracosm that they had created and shared together. At 21 George was handsome, athletic, and brilliant: full of promise. Both family and friends saw the strong presence of Arthur in George; so did Barrie. He had begun to rely on the strength and masculinity of George as a guide for the boys and for Barrie himself. The letters exchanged between them during the war before George's death show the unique quality of their relationship. Barrie demonstrates an almost frantic parental concern, which is mingled with a maternal touch and the delicacy of a lover. In one letter Barrie writes:

> Hoping for another letter as soon as you have the time. You should see how I plunge thro' my letter-bag looking for one from you. It is almost too exciting, and I have some bad nights, I can tell you. . . . Wherever you are, I hope you see near your bed the flowers I want to place there in a nice vase, and the illustrated papers, and a new work by Compton MacKenzie which I read aloud to you! I shall be so anxious till I get another line from you (Birkin, 1979, p. 235).

George's letters to Barrie are reassuring as he tries to relieve his "uncle's" anxiety, as demonstrated in this last letter to Barrie: "Meanwhile, dear Uncle Jim, you must carry on with your job of keeping up your courage. I will write every time I come out of action." Barrie never saw George again, but four days before his death, George received Uncle Jim's last letter:

> [I am] more and more wishing you were a girl of 21 instead of a boy, so that I could say the things to you that are now always in my heart. For four years [since Sylvia's death] I have been waiting for you to become 21 and a little more, so that we could get closer and closer to each other, without

> any words needed. . . . I just want your-self. There may be moments when a knowledge of all you are to me will make you a little more careful, and so I can't help going on saying these things (p. 242).

Peter Davies records the memory of hearing "an eerie Banshee wail" from Barrie when he received the news of George's death. It was devastating to Barrie. This was the little boy who had once personified the magic youth and the spirit of creativity for Barrie. As a child, George had told him, "To die will be an awfully big adventure." Barrie had given those exact words to Peter Pan as the tide begins to cover him in Mermaid Lagoon. Now Barrie deleted them from the manuscript. The harsh reality of death, of loss, of war intruded itself into Barrie's world. But he still had Michael.

Perhaps the most talented, sensitive, brilliant, and beautiful of all the Davies boys, Michael had demonstrated special problems from early childhood. Even while his parents were alive, he experienced severe nightmares and sleep-walking. This continued into adolescence, when he was a student at Eton. Michael and Barrie were very close; when away at school, Michael wrote to Barrie every night and received daily letters from him. Just as Margaret Ogilvy had saved all of her son's letters, now that son preserved all of Michael's letters, keeping the latest letter under his sheet. Barrie was enormously solicitous of Michael, who was moody and brooding; unlike the outgoing and gregarious George, Michael turned inward and wrote poetry.

After George's death, Michael became even more important to Barrie. He began working on a murder play to please Michael, who had first suggested it. Clearly the relationship was reciprocal, and Michael's priority was to please his guardian-parent, which he did by matriculating at Oxford instead of going to Paris. Yet Michael wanted his independence, and after a year at Oxford determined he would attend the University of Paris the following autumn. In his inimitable fashion, Barrie rented an entire island for the summer holiday; he was determined it would be spectacular—and perhaps Michael would change his mind.

Though part of Barrie had died with the deaths of the three members of the Davies family, especially George, he could still create. His drama *Mary Rose* (1920) was a great success. It is the story of a young mother who disappears on an island in the Outer Hebrides and returns years later to find her son. A reversal of Peter Pan, *Mary Rose* remains the same age as the day she died while the son grows into a man, and thus she cannot recognize him. Barrie's themes and his search are the same. Now the one-act murder play that he had completed for Michael (*Shall We Join the Ladies?*) would have a glittering first-night performance as a tribute to Michael on his twenty-first birthday. But Michael never reached that birthday.

Six years after George's death, Michael, age 20, drowned with a fellow student, Rupert Buxford, at Sanford Pool, Oxford. The circumstances were obscure. Michael was terrified of water and had never mastered the skill of swimming.

Many people, including Michael's brother, Nico, thought it had been a suicide, perhaps a death pact with Buxford. Witnesses said the young men's bodies were entwined and there had been no struggle. It shattered Barrie. His friends feared he would take his own life. Later he wrote, "Michael was pretty much my world, he had been the one great thing in my life for many years" (Birkin, 1979, p. 295). The reality of this further great loss destroyed the creativity in Barrie.

Once more, in the last year of his life, Barrie attempted to write. At age 77, the old themes were still present in his last play, *The Boy David.* The title and his choice of material brought him full circle to the idealized dead brother, David; to the boy David in *The Little White Bird,* who was George Llewelyn Davies; to his Michael, also dead at the threshold of manhood; to the eternal boy, Peter Pan; and finally to Barrie himself. The vision was gone: the play was an absolute failure.

"To have faith is to have wings," said Barrie in *The Little White Bird.* With the death of Michael, Barrie's wings were clipped forever. He had lost his muses, the objects of his romantic ideation, those ideal images which had shared the magic of his paracosms. The Davies family, especially George, Michael, and Sylvia, had given Barrie the opportunity to explore those idealized images that early in his life had formulated a part of his own identity. Now reality could not be denied: that very reality that Barrie had assiduously avoided. For his desire always to be a little boy and not to grow up was more than a rich imaginative mode of perception and exploration; it was also an avoidance of the inevitable pain attached to the knowledge that Barrie knew he could never function as an adult male. With "his boys," youth was still eternal, but when he lost them, he also lost a vital part of himself. The creative thrust was now gone and so was the magical path to Neverland.

CHAPTER 8

Isak Dinesen: Romantic Ideation and the Quest for Self

> If I know a song of Africa . . . of the Giraffe, and the African new moon lying on her back . . . does Africa know a song of me? Would the air over the plain quiver with a colour that I had had on, or the children invent a game in which my name was, or the full moon throw a shadow over the gravel of the drive that was like me, or would the eagles of Ngong look out for me?
>
> *Out of Africa*
>
> Isak D inesen (1885-1962)

Isak Dinesen (the pen name for Karen Blixen) engaged in romantic ideation her entire life. It began with her relationship with her father, Wilhelm Dinesen. According to writer-critic Georg Brandes, Wilhelm was an elusive, passionate, and rather troubled man, always in search of "a more intense experience of his being" (Thurman, 1982, p. 13). War temporarily satisfied this need. It took him away from his personal problems and placed him on the edge of existence. This was the Dano-Prussian War of 1864, in which Denmark lost a third of its territory and two-fifths of its population. Later, in 1870, Wilhelm Dinesen enlisted as a captain in the French army when the Prussians attacked France. After that war, he, like Wordsworth, turned to Nature for consolation and peace. He also demonstrated a romanticism, which would touch his daughter Karen profoundly.

At 25 Wilhelm Dinesen fell in love with his cousin, Agnes Frijs, 18, who died two years later from typhoid. Though he shared an aristocratic heritage with Agnes, they were not social equals, and he never could have married her, but her untimely death intensified his feelings for her. In his writings on passion, Wilhelm states that the deepest loves are aroused by what one can never have. His daughter Karen would later echo these words in her own writings.

After Agnes' death, Wilhelm Dinesen sailed to North America: traveling from Quebec to Chicago, he later settled in Wisconsin, living alone in a log cabin, baking his own bread, surviving on his hunting and fishing skills, trading with the Indians. He named the cabin Frydenlund, after one of the houses in Agnes Frijs's family. The Chippewa named him Boganis (hazelnut), which he later took as his *nom de plum*. He was sexually active with the Indian women, which apparently led to his developing syphilis.

Wilhelm Dinesen greatly admired the Indians for their knowledge and reverence for Nature, their bravery and honor code. "Their eyes see more than ours," he would tell Karen, "[they] are better than our civilized people of Europe." He told Karen many tales of his adventures with the Indians. His attitude toward them would be reflected later in Karen's attitude toward the Africans in Kenya.

Wilhelm continued his pattern of restlessness. He returned to Denmark before his mother's impending death; he then departed for Europe after his father's death two years later. When the Crimean War began, he went to Turkey, hoping to fight against the Russians. In his *Letters from the Hunt* he evokes some erotic adventures in Constantinople (Istanbul). Unsettled and discontented, he would later write, "Love and Peace hate, persecute, and annihilate one another" (Thurman, 1982, p. 21).

Wilhelm Dinesen was 35, Ingeborg Westenholz, 24, when he proposed marriage. Dominated by Mama Westenholz, a huge cadre of Westenholz women surrounded Ingeborg's first child, Inger. Cast aside and overwhelmed by this enormous female presence, Wilhelm went hunting and promised himself that the next child would be "his." That next child was Karen, or Tanne, as she was called. Karen was the only one of five siblings (three girls, two boys) who became extremely close to her father. Wilhelm led his daughter out of the domestic, feminine circle and into the world. He introduced her to a Nature that he worshipped. They went for long walks in the woods: noting wildflowers and grasses, listening to bird songs; heightening her senses; making her as conscious of them as a hunter: all of which became an invaluable preparation for Isak Dinesen, the writer. It was a man's world, and he had chosen her to share it with him.

And Wilhelm told her stories of his life: his military campaigns, his sojourn in Wisconsin, his solitary life at Frydenlund; his experiences with various tribes of American Indians. More importantly, he infused his beliefs and his attitudes toward people and toward life into his young daughter. He shared his ideas with her as he was writing *Letters from the Hunt:* notions that both hunting and loving are "mortal" struggles and both are forms of play (Thurman, 1982, p. 27).

Karen spoke of her father's total acceptance of and love for her as a small child. She adored him and didn't want to share her intimacy with him with anyone. She took pride in being her father's girl, not "theirs"—her term for the Westenholz women. Wilhelm confided in her, treated her like an adult, shared confidences with her, especially when he was troubled. That is why Karen was devastated at the age of ten when her father committed suicide.

Karen's attitude toward the Westenholz women was very negative. Her grandmother, Mama Wenstenholz, never accepted Wilhelm as "suitable" for her daughter, though she retained a polite civility. The young Karen sensed this and, identifying with her father, stated, "My grandmother did not like me. She liked my sisters better" (Langbaum, 1964, p. 39).

Forty years later, Isak Dinesen wrote the story "Alkmene" (*Winter's Tales*), which emulated these family experiences. Alkmene, a beautiful six-year-old orphan, is adopted into a simple family that loves her but cannot understand her. The girl demonstrates aristocratic traits, later corroborated by her inheritance from an unknown source. Alkmene, seeking her identity, runs away from this family who will not permit her to follow "her destiny." Her friend, Vilhelm, tells her, "But your folks love you . . . if you will only agree to stay with them." Alkmene replies, "What about the children, Vilhelm, who do not want to be loved?" (Dinesen, 1993, p. 205).

Vilhelm is another autobiographical component of Dinesen's story, in the relationship between him and Alkmene. An aristocratic boy, eight years older than Alkmene, he shares her esthetic qualities and values: they understand each other. But Vilhelm does not "save her" from her fate: the bourgeois milieu in which she is forced to live. The relationship between Alkmene and Vilhelm parallels the bond between Karen and Wilhelm—even Isak Dinesen's choice of names is revealing. The bond is close, intimate, asexual: the two are separated by age and experience. Too late, Vilhelm realizes the mistake he has made in abandoning Alkmene. Her ending is tragic because she has never felt fulfilled or whole.

While her father was with her, Karen Dinesen could dismiss "her mother's family," but when she lost him, she, too, felt abandoned. In Wilhelm's suicide note to his wife, Ingeborg, he wrote that the two other girls would fend for themselves, "but my heart aches for little Tanne." Karen (Tanne) felt an enormous guilt that somehow she was powerless to dissuade Wilhelm from his ultimate fate: he hanged himself from the rafters of his apartment.

His choice of how he would commit suicide is curious because he was a military officer: hanging was the fate of deserters. He and Karen both shared the same last emotion: tremendous guilt. Later, Dinesen writes, "I think my greatest misfortune was Father's death. Father understood me as I was, although I was so young, and loved me for myself." While Mama and Aunt Bess "are always trying to change me into something quite different. They do not like the parts of me that I believe to be good" (Dinesen, 1981, p. 110). In Dinesen's story, Alkmene echoes Karen's feelings.

Wilhelm's son Thomas believed his father had been suffering from syphilis. Ironically, when he shared this revelation with Karen, years later, she herself was suffering from syphilis. "My father's destiny," she said, "has, curiously enough, to a great extent, been repeated in my own" (Thurman, 1982, p. 53).

Karen grieved for her father, even into adolescence; she thought "constantly" about her father and felt his absence from her life as an intolerable tragedy. At the age of 15, in a letter, she makes a passionate plea to him:

> My dear and beloved friend, my wise and gentle brother:
>
> If you had been on earth still, I should have come to you and you would have taught me to love and to approach thine [*sic*] light, but you are gone away to high worlds, I know not where you dwell, spirit that I love. But do not leave me alone, if your spirit dwells still sometimes on earth, where you loved and suffered, let it dwell within me, who love [*sic*] you. And give me only once a token that you live and are the same, and that my spirit could reach thine, and if you give it to me, I shall follow your footsteps and be you disciple, today and always. Perhaps I shall be it in all cases, but know, my brother, how hard it is to be alone, be with me, and give me your bless [*sic*] dear beloved brother, my master, my teacher, my dearest friend (p. 53).

It is significant that this letter was written in English, a foreign language to Karen, but a foreign language can provide distance and thus protect one's emotions. It can also ensure privacy.

This letter is also a remarkable example of Karen's romantic ideation of her father. She literally attempts to merge her identity with Wilhelm, to become him in order to possess his characteristics. His wisdom, his power, shall be hers. She will not feel so vulnerable; she will not be alone. Her choice of words to address Wilhelm reveals her feelings toward him: dear beloved brother, my master and teacher, dearest friend, wise and gentle brother. Theirs was a relationship that transcended father and daughter in an intimate and interdependent way, for Karen becomes Wilhelm's protector even as he empowers and protects her. And in their merging, Karen becomes both personas. That sense of union extended into her later life. At 36, when her marriage and her farm were both foundering, she wrote to her mother, "If I can make something of myself again, and can look at life calmly and clearly one day—then it is Father who has done it for me. It is his blood and his mind that will bring me through it. Often I get the feeling that he is beside me, helping me, many times by saying: 'Don't give a damn about it'" (Dinesen, 1981, p. 110).

The ultimate end of romantic ideation is mysticism. In Karen's responses to her father at 15 and at 36, she seeks this merging of their spirits. At 64, she attempts this same process with the poet Thorkild Bjornvig. And she engaged in romantic ideation for the remainder of her life. From her father, the process continued into her marriage, and into her writing.

Though Bror von Blixen became Karen's husband, it was his twin brother, Hans, with whom Karen fell madly in love at age 24. Hans, who raced horses and airplanes, rejected her, and Bror was not interested in her either until he realized that she was passionately in love with Hans. Then he assiduously courted her.

Hans' rejection was very difficult for Karen. Her maxim was that the final word as to what one is worth lies with the opposite sex. So it was Bror whom Karen accepted as her husband, after his third proposal. Her family fought the engagement; her friends questioned her integrity in marrying the twin of the man she really loved. All of this made her more tenacious in her decision to marry Bror von Blixen and to leave Denmark for Africa.

In Africa, Karen Blixen's masculine identity blossomed: she shoots lions; she becomes the natives' teacher-doctor; she is in charge of her coffee farm. Bror was frequently absent and it was Karen who made the decisions. In a letter to her mother in 1921, she writes, "there is something in the way I love you that resembles the way Father loved you . . . and so you must allow me to write to you as you would have allowed Father to write" (Dinesen, 1981, p. 111).

Later, in *Out of Africa,* her love of and affinity for Nature reflect the lessons she learned from Wilhelm. Her descriptions of her farm in Kenya read like poetry:

> The colors were dry and burnt, like the colors in pottery . . .
> The tall solitary trees [possessed] a heroic and romantic
> air like full rigged ships with their sails clewed up, and to
> the edge of a wood a strange appearance as if the whole
> wood were faintly vibrating (Dinesen, 1937, p. 3).

Karen Blixen owned 6000 acres of land; 600 acres were planted in coffee. Part of the farm was native forest, and about 1000 acres were squatters' land, or *shambas.* Native Africans, she writes, "hold a few acres on a white man's farm, and in return have to work for him a certain number of days in the year." She had a great affection for the natives: "The discovery of the dark races was to me a magnificent enlargement of all my world" (p. 17). Her relationships with the native Africans paralleled Wilhelm's experiences with the Wisconsin Indians:

> I have met the eyes of my Native companions. It made me reflect that perhaps they were, in life itself, within their own element such as we can never be, like fishes in deep water. . . . This assurance, this art of swimming, they had . . . because they had preserved a knowledge that was lost to us by our first parents (p. 19).

Karen also adopts some of her father's philosophy when she writes, "Africa . . . will teach you: that God and the Devil are one, the majesty coeternal, not two uncreated but one uncreated" (p. 20). This concept appears and reappears in much of her work, just as it appeared in Wilhelm's *Letters from the Hunt.* Isak Dinesen illustrates this duality in her story "The Monkey" in *Seven Gothic Tales.* She describes the Wendish Idol, the goddess of love, who had the face and the façade of a beautiful woman, but when she is turned around, the back of the idol is an image of a monkey. In the story, this is further illustrated in the transformation of the Virgin Prioress into a monkey. Her own monkey from Zanzibar takes her place as Prioress—with a decidedly wicked character—and she becomes a very docile monkey. It was years later that Dinesen would write from her experiences. Now, in Africa, she confronted Bror's behavior as her mother had witnessed Wilhelm's in Denmark.

Many of Wilhelm Dinesen's characteristics, including a pattern of enormous restlessness, were shared by Bror, Baron von Blixen. The consummate hunter, farming bored him and he was constantly on safari. He loved living on the edge: he drank heavily, gambled excessively, and was sexually promiscuous. There were a variety of affairs with women from the Muthiaga Club, but von Blixen never hid the fact that he slept with native women, and syphilis was almost epidemic among the Masai. He possessed a charismatic charm that people responded to. It was Bror, not his twin, Hans, who became a romantic legend in Africa. He was immortalized as Robert Wilson in Hemingway's "The Short Happy Life of Francis Macomber," and was worshipped for his enormous courage and spirit by Beryl Markham in her book *West with the Night* (1983). Bror von Blixen was the standard by which hunters were measured. Karen loved this aspect of Bror, and she loved being the "Baroness," a corroboration of her identity with Wilhelm Dinesen and his aristocratic heritage.

It was Bror who taught her how to shoot. He took her on a safari with him, and she loved it—even the skinning of the lion down to his "elegant bones." It was Bror who gave her syphilis, a fact long hidden in her earlier biographies. Karen's syphilis and Bror's affairs did not help the marriage. Bror left the house in 1919, involved with Cockie Birbeck, who would become his second wife. Karen, too, had affairs, but she didn't want the divorce. She wanted stability, the respectability of marriage, and she wanted to retain her title. When Bror divorced her in 1922, she told her mother and begged her not to tell the rest of the family. She asked her mother, Ingeborg, to "talk about me to Father. It is really he who is responsible for he deserted me, and must have seen that things were not going to be easy for me" (Dinesen, 1981, p. 111). An interesting detail in the divorce proceedings is that Karen shaved five years from her age, but that didn't help her depression. "Bror," she said, "has been the person I was closest to in the world," and she felt as if she had lost a child. Though she never spoke to Cockie, she and Bror remained friends.

It was in 1918 that Karen Blixen met Denys Finch-Hatton. He, too, was a superb hunter; he frequently went on safari with Bror, who would laughingly introduce him as "my friend and my wife's lover." A year after the divorce, Finch-Hatton moved his things to the farm.

Denys Finch-Hatton was the great romance of Karen's life. Adored by everyone at Eton, enormously successful at Oxford, worshipped in Africa, his charm, wit, and intellect were tremendously admired. Like Wilhelm, like Bror, Denys came and went frequently; he, too, was restless. In eight years of living together, he and Karen actually spent only two years and two months together. The constant separation heightened their passion: a blatant definition of romantic love. They never dealt with reality, and Karen catered to his every wish. He enriched her life with music and poetry; he gave her a new perspective of Africa from his small plane, a Gypsy Moth. Good food, fine wines, stimulating conversation: these were the things they shared. Denys became Karen's muse. He loved a good story, and she would write them in her head to recite them for him when he returned to her farm. Later, Isak Dinesen would transform them into print.

Midway in their relationship, Karen (age 41) thought she was pregnant. She cabled Denys, using the code name Daniel for the child. Denys replied, "Strongly urge you to cancel Daniel's visit." A second cable read, "Do as you like about Daniel as I should welcome him if I could offer partnership but this is impossible" (Thurman, 1982, p. 208). Given her age and medical history, Karen probably had a miscarriage: Daniel was never born. This was a reality she could not ignore. Nor was the loss of her farm. Never economically viable, the coffee farm finally folded. Again, Finch-Hatton refused to help her: no offer of marriage, no arrangement for her economic security. She would return to Denmark, to her mother's house. She and Denys quarreled: he took back his ring. It was Beryl Markham whom Finch-Hatton invited to accompany him to Voi, his final and fatal flight in his Gypsy Moth. At first Markham accepted, then refused because her flight instructor (Tom Black) had a "bad feeling" about her going (Markham, 1983, p. 194).

Ironically, it was only in Finch-Hatton' death that Karen finally possessed him. She picked his grave site, a place they had once chosen, presided at his funeral; she acted as the significant woman in his life and changed the stories of their last moments together, as documented in her autobiographical story, *Out of Africa.* But this romantic ideation was not enough. She attempted suicide, slashing her wrists in a friend's house before she left Africa. She also left a suicide note, which has since vanished from the Blixen archives. Though she lost a lot of blood, her attempt served as a catharsis from her excruciating pain. It is not insignificant that Karen attempted to replicate her father's demise.

Wilhelm Dinesen was the idealized male model whom Karen repeatedly sought to find. Her choices of Bror von Blixenand Denys Finch-Hatton reflected her narcissistic needs. She projected onto these men what she felt she wanted, needed, to be complete. What she desired from both men was intimacy, a commitment that even her father had not given her. Had she transcended her narcissistic needs, she might have observed that neither Bror nor Denys possessed or desired a capacity for intimacy or commitment. The two men had much in common: their physical prowess as hunters; their courage; their independence from convention; their need for adventure and solitude; their reluctance for commitment in relationships. Isak Dinesen transforms memory into fiction; it is a blatant transition—especially in terms of her relationship with Finch-Hatton.

The men were obvious in their words and actions. Karen saw and responded to what she *wished* to see. Bror was uncultivated and rough beside Denys, but she fought the divorce because she felt vulnerable, abandoned. With Denys, the scenario was repeated. Things went well until she needed him. The possession, the control that she desperately sought, always evaded her—until she met Thorkild Bjornvig.

Thorkild Bjornvig, a young Danish poet, entered Karen Blixen's life when she was 64 years old, living in Denmark and experiencing a "period of great starkness in her life" (Thurman, 1982, p. 335). The more a "productive dimension" eluded her in her own writing, the more she considered turning Bjornvig into a poet. "Imperfect and incomplete alone, together they would be a unity" (p. 335). Once more Karen is engaged in romantic ideation, searching for the male to bring her to perfection. She and the poet formed a pact, a mystical union, a vow of eternal love. Bjornvig would justify her efforts by becoming a first-class poet, by bringing glory to them both.

Karen Blixen began by trying to make Thorkild Bjornvig "a man of the world"—like her father or Finch-Hatton. This relationship lasted for four years. Though Bjornvig had a wife and son, Karen repeatedly claimed him; he lived in her house for months at a time. She dominated him; played God with his life; caressed and bullied him simultaneously; spoke of leaving Rungstedlund (her family estate) to him if he would live with her. When Bjornvig fell in love with a young woman, Karen felt betrayed, both as a woman and as his "God." When the affair ended, Bjornvig returned to his wife and attempted to break the pact with Karen. The following is an excerpt from the pact.

> You shall belong to no one and to nothing, to no party, to no majority, to no minority, to no society except in that it serves me at my altar. You shall not belong to your parents, nor to your wife nor children, nor to your brothers and sisters, nor to them who speak your language, nor to those who speak any other—and best of all to thine own self. You shall belong only to *me* in this world (Thurman, 1982, p. 336).

Karen Blixen signed this document and gave it to Thorkild Bjornvig. In one of their last meetings, on a walk, they encountered a snake lying in the sun. It did not move as they approached it. How each construed the snake as symbol defines their relationship. Karen saw it as a good omen, something to protect them both from good and evil. Bjornvig saw it as an indication of Karen's satanic power over him. He wrote his final goodbye to her, and she accepted it. But she did not completely relinquish her control over him. She used him in her fiction.

Like most writers, Isak Dinesen exploited her experiences and transformed them into her tales. In "The Dreamers" (*Seven Gothic Tales,* 1934), she created Pellegrina Leoni, a great opera diva who allegedly died in a theater fire in Milan 13 years before the story begins. In fact, Pellegrina recovered from the burns, but she lost her voice and would never sing again. She insisted on a burial service, and the world believed her to be buried in a little cemetery in Milan. She had attempted suicide and now felt that Pellegrina was indeed dead. "I will not be one person again. I will be always many persons from now. Never again will I have my heart and my whole life bound up with one woman, to suffer so much" (Dinesen, 1934, p. 345).

Pellegrina admonishes her Jewish friend, Marcus, "Be many people." And she does precisely that: she becomes Ollala who inhabits an Italian brothel; she is also Madame Lola, a milliner by day and a revolutionist by night; she is also a religious martyr named Madame Rosalba. Three men fall in love with her—one with each female character—and when they tell each other their stories, they all describe "their woman" as the possessor of a deep, white scar from her left ear to her collarbone who is followed by a very wealthy, elderly Jew. When each man tries to possess her, or force her into a fixed identity, she disappears.

Pellegrina's rejection of self, of identity, evolves from her excruciating pain: the loss of her beautiful voice, which defined her. Knowing who she is and who she was, she consciously assumes many identities. In becoming all of these women, she is none of them. She has traded the myth of Pellegrina for a series of mythic women, none of whom really exist; she is spiritually dead.

When Pellegrina is discovered by her three former lovers, she throws herself from a precipice and loses consciousness. When she awakes, she is Pellegrina, the opera diva, and she attempts to finish the aria of "Don Giovanni" that she was singing on the night of the fire. She has returned to herself.

Karen Blixen admitted that Pellegrina represented herself; that the loss of the diva's voice by fire symbolized the loss of her farm. This loss probably extended to Denys Finch-Hatton, to her broken marriage, and even to her father, Wilhelm. Her "loss" was inextricably bound to these men to whom she looked for her own identity. The romantic ideation in her life evolved into her fiction.

Later, Pellegrina Leoni becomes the focal point for Karen's relationship with Thorkild Bjornvig, the young Danish poet. Karen admitted that his violent rejection of her possessiveness formed the basis of her story "Echoes" (*Last Tales,* 1957). The theme again deals with romantic ideation, with the possession of the qualities of the idealized romantic figure.

Pellegrina no longer has a voice, but she finds a young boy, Emanuele, who sings like an angel. When she first hears him sing "The Magnificat" in the church of a small Italian village, her reaction to his voice is powerful: "Her body fell from her like a garment, because her soul went straight upwards with the tones, for the voice that gave them out was known to her. It was the voice of young Pellegrina Leoni" (Dinesen, 1957, p. 167). Emanuele represents a part of herself that she thought was lost forever. He becomes her muse to recreate the voice of the young Pellegrina, but it is a narcissistic love that is demanding and possessive. Should she lose him, once again she would lose that part of herself that centered her identity.

Pellegrina takes Emanuele as her pupil. Knowing that his voice will break within three or four years, she is determined to train him so that "The voice of Pellegrina should be heard again by the world, in that heavenly *da capo* which is also called resurrection" (p. 170). Pellegrina works intensely with Emanuele; she feels that she has made him ageless, and she becomes ageless as well. She perceives that his face takes on a resemblance to her own.

> She felt her own lungs drawing breath in his body and his tongue in her own mouth . . . she made him talk and made his eyes meet hers, and she sensed, as she had often done before, the power of her beauty and her mind over a young male being. Her heart cried out in triumph: "I have got my talons in him. He will not escape me (p. 172).

And later, as he grew, she thought, "In three years we two will be one, and you will be my lover, Emanuele" (p. 176).

Pellegrina's possession will be completed when she also sexually rules Emanuele. He will become her voice, the manifestation of her talent, her creativity, her genius. At first there is reciprocation between the two. At the end of one lesson Pellegrina thinks she would die if she lost Emanuele. At this moment the boy expresses her thoughts: "If you were to die, I should die too." It is the epitome of romantic ideation: Cathy and Heathcliff; Tristan and Isolde; Romeo and Juliet. But death is not what separates them: it is Pellegrina's request to mix their blood.

Dinesen, the author, justifies Pellegrina's request, saying that Pellegrina was attempting to "cure" Emanuele's fear of physical pain. He submits to her needle, pricking three of his fingers. Wiping the drops of blood on her handkerchief, she lifts it to her lips and sucks the blood. The next day Emanuele does not come for his lesson. When he returns to her, she tells him, "you are now singing with my own voice . . . you have got Pellegrina Leoni's voice in your chest" (p. 181).

Emanuele abandons his voice teacher and she pursues him. Fighting for his freedom, his identity, he screams, "You are a witch. You are a vampire. You are wanting to drink my blood. Now I know that I should die if I went back to you" (pp. 185-186). But Pellegrina is relentless in her pursuit of Emanuele. She finally desists when he hits her with a large stone, drawing blood from her head. It is only his violent action that enables him to free himself from her possession.

Pellegrina needs Emanuele to be whole, to be vital. First, she idealizes him, and then she needs to possess him. There is also an inherent narcissism here, because Pellegrina doesn't think or care about Emanuele as a person, but as an extension of herself.

As Pellegrina reflects on Emanuele's rebellion, she rationalizes her behavior, focusing on his ignorance of the meaning of the "mingling of blood," which she defines as "longing to give all my own blood to you." But then in a moment of startling insight, she says, "And then, maybe, he was not as much mistaken as all that" (p. 188).

When Thorkild Bjornvig broke off his relationship with Karen Blixen, she pursued him. Inviting him to Rungstedlund, she asked him to renew their pact, and she wanted them to sign it in their blood. "Blood is thicker than words," she said. Horrified, Bjornvig would not agree to what he thought was satanic madness. After this turning point in their relationship, Karen "fell into a black depression."

The parallels between Karen Blixen's life and her art, the tale of "Echoes," are poignant. Possessing Bjornvig made her ageless, just as Pellegrina was ageless with Emanuele. The difference in age and experience was relevant to both. Karen wanted Bjornvig to carry "her voice" to posterity: possessing him would give her life. At first reciprocal in their romantic ideation, Bjornvig, like Emanuele, finally fought for his freedom and his identity: he severed their relationship.

Thus the theme of romantic ideation permeates the writing as well as the life of Karen Blixen. While the men in her life whom she wished to possess finally eluded her—her father; her husband, Bror; her lover, Denys Finch-Hatton; and the young poet, Thorkild Bjornvig—she possessed a portion of all of them in her writing as she sought out the idealized male figure as a way to make herself complete.

The power of a childhood loss touched Isak Dinesen's life profoundly. The romantic ideation of her father, arrested and perpetuated because of his death, led to an identity with him that transferred to her relationships with Bror von Blixen, Denys Finch-Hatton, and Thorkild Bjornvig. Her subsequent creativity was another intense search for wholeness in her own identity.

CHAPTER 9

Jack Kerouac: Saints and Fallen Angels

I've seen a vision. And the way Cody stands there not saying a word with his arms outstretched for some reason, struck a pose of some sort to surprise us or warn us, he's so much like St. Michael.

Big Sur
Jack Kerouac (1922-1969)

MEMORY'S CHILD

It is probably significant that one definition of "beat" was coined by an influential San Francisco columnist, Herb Caen, while another definition is attributed to Jack Kerouac (Nicosia, 1994, p. 468). The two definitions differ significantly. Herb Caen was contrasting this literary movement with the "Lost Generation" that he was familiar with. For Caen and the popular press, the "beats" were just that—far out and defeated by the demands of life and quick to find alternative satisfaction in sex and drugs. In contrast, Kerouac saw his generation as consumed by a beautiful, peaceful view of life, struggling toward a vision that would match their spiritual wish. They were beatific, and the poems and fiction of his friends would be an invigorating spiritual alternative to the prosaic, material concerns of the Eisenhower years. Kerouac was preoccupied with spiritual visions.

Kerouac's background was French-Canadian. This writer who was to have considerable influence on American literature was, in effect, the son of immigrants. His father, Leo, and his mother, Gabrielle, were born in Quebec and came from strong French-Catholic backgrounds. One of the first jobs that Leo had was as a reporter and typesetter for a French newspaper in Nashua. Not long after their marriage Leo and Gabrielle moved to the textile-manufacturing town of Lowell, Massachusetts. While Leo started his own print shop, Gabrielle had three children: Gerard in 1917, Caroline in 1920, and Jack in 1922. Gabrielle was intensely religious, and Kerouac's early memories were fused with the spiritual order of the doctrine of the Catholic Church and stories of the saints. Over time, his memories of his childhood became laden with sadness, guilt, associations with death, and "Gloomy Lowell" (Kerouac, 1987, 1991).

Although Leo spoke some English, Gabrielle could not, and French was spoken in the home. Jack Kerouac did not learn to speak and write English until he was five years old, and he used his native French-Canadian language throughout his life. At about the time he was learning the English language at his Catholic school, he was going through a major reaction to the death of his nine-year-old brother, Gerard. Gerard was considered a saint by his mother and by the nuns who taught both Gerard and Jack. His death from rheumatic heart disease was long, painful, and fully witnessed by the young Jack. The family never recovered from his death. As Kerouac later wrote, his mother lost all her teeth and his father lost his Catholic faith. Working through his own mourning and tremendous sense of guilt, Kerouac, as a child, developed the "Great World Snake" fantasy and the sense that he was Judas to the Christ-like figure of Gerard. The evil serpent's purpose in life was to come from the dead, find Kerouac, and destroy him. He struggled with these images of himself by attempting to reduce his parents' grief and his own anxiety and guilt by being the idealized Gerard. Leo's printing shop was destroyed in the great Merrimack Flood of 1936 and he never recovered financially. Jack Kerouac tried especially hard to be the successful son his unsuccessful father needed. He was a source of family pride, as he was an outstanding football player and something of a high school hero in Lowell, where he grew up. Although his own memories of this time describe his guilty sexual preoccupations and obsession with death, outwardly he was a star high school running back and an admired intellect among his blue-collar friends. The severe tensions between self and ideal culminated after he received a football scholarship to Columbia University to be coached by the then famous Lou Little. Drawn more to the escape of movies and literature than to the classroom and competitive sports, Kerouac soon dropped out of school.

This brief period of time, between 1941 and 1944 (Clark, 1990), marks the point in Kerouac's life when he began his effort to break with his failed identification with Gerard and his painful memories of place: "Beaulieu-street where I learned to cry and be scared of the dark and my brother for many years . . ." (Kerouac, 1987, p. 38). He tried to be the athlete Leo wanted, but he was never able to meet the academic demands as well as physical commitment required to play football at a major university. As his college career collapsed he entered into close friendship with individuals who were gay. Kerouac's involvement in a murder that included two of his gay friends was major news in the New York newspapers. Where a year before Leo and Gabrielle could read about their son's outstanding and admired skills as a running back, they now read about his role as a material witness in a sordid murder. Kerouac had helped dispose of the murder weapon and the victim's glasses. The newspaper reports stressed the homosexual relationships of the young men, and Leo was so disgusted with his son that he refused to post bond to get him out of jail. In order to get out of jail Kerouac promised marriage to a woman he had been dating, Edie Parker. She would find the money if he would marry her. He agreed, and she got the money from her wealthy parents. The marriage lasted two months.

Another indication of Kerouac's confused state during this time is that before his involvement in the murder and his brief marriage, he had impulsively enlisted in the Navy. While in boot camp he hit an officer, and during a drill he laid down his rifle and walked off the field to the library. He was soon placed in a psychiatric unit. While there he developed the fantasy that he could see through another man's head, and one morning, completely naked, he bolted out of the unit and ran the length of a nearby battalion field, yelling "Geronimo!" He was soon discharged with a diagnosis of schizoid personality with "angel tendencies" (Nicosia, 1994, p. 106).

The term "angel tendencies" used at that time meant an unrealistic tendency toward self-aggrandizement. There was a schizoid split in Kerouac's personality during this crisis, and while hospitalized he probably expressed the need to see himself differently and in more self-accepting terms as he painfully realized that, in this life, he could not obtain the angelic state of grace eternally possessed by his dead brother. It is telling that years later he looked back on his brief career in the Navy as a betrayal of his youthful dream to be a real "American Man" (Nicosia, 1994, p. 106). Although previously Kerouac was interested in writing, his serious attempts to write began at this time, as he attempted to break with the past in his new relationships. William Burroughs and Neal Cassady were to have a tremendous influence on Kerouac's life and creativity. The two entered his life at a time when he had lost his sense of purpose, and his relationships with them represent Kerouac's effort to replace the gloomy guilt-ridden memories of the past represented by Gerard and the Catholic faith of his mother. Life was known through suffering. Cassady especially served as an idealized "brother" who was Kerouac's muse and guide to an alternative way of dealing with the encounters of life and death. For Cassady, the past did not matter and life was nothing to be afraid of.

Much of Kerouac's fiction is based on his own experiences with his friends or, more precisely, his somewhat removed observation of those experiences. However, his interpretations of his past, usually the time before he met Cassady, also appear in his fiction, and when this occurs Kerouac's memory of the teachings of Gerard's life and death dominate. A major life-determining theme appears: what moves the living brother of Gerard in understanding death is not its eminence but the nostalgic memory of it.

THE ACTUAL TRUTH

Kerouac published his first book, *The Town and the City,* in 1950. He started working on a story immediately after the death of his father, and the book reflects the influences of the writing style of Thomas Wolfe. It received less than supportive reviews by the critics, and sales were low. Kerouac was depressed about the response to his book. His confidence in his ability to write was faltering when he received a letter from Neal Cassady in which Neal tells the story of *Christmas of 1946 Denver* with his girlfriends Joan Anderson and Cherry Mary. Kerouac had known Neal for approximately four years, and they had shared the travels that were to become *On The Road* (Kerouac, 1976). Kerouac immediately read Cassady's stories and was profoundly moved. Shortly afterwards he wrote a series of letters to Cassady that demonstrate how influential Cassady's style of writing became for Kerouac. After one of the letters from Cassady, which was a 13,000-word story of his relationship with the two women, Kerouac wrote that it was "the best thing ever written in America" and compared it with *Notes from the Underground* by Dostoevsky (Charters, 1995, p. 242). In his writings and his life, Cassady impressed Kerouac by his authenticity and truthfulness. Kerouac wrote back saying that he needed to confess to Neal his own hypocrisy and dishonesty with self and at the same time write what was to be his lifework (p. 243). In the first series of long letters to Cassady, Kerouac attempted to "proceed to the actual truth" of his life.

Kerouac begins with his memory of his own birth and the images of "red air and sadness." Remembering himself in a wicker-basket baby carriage, he thinks that somewhere during that time his sin began, as he knew that the Great World Snake was worming its way after him. In this context Kerouac moves on to describe Gerard, his dead brother. While Kerouac describes mankind as "covered with sin and self disgrace," Gerard is a beautiful, angelic boy who, according to Kerouac, looks like himself in his earliest photographs. He goes on to write that Gerard could not understand or tolerate violence of any kind. At one time Gerard lectured their cat for eating a mouse. Kerouac tells of his mother repeating such stories of Gerard to him a million times, and in his words he "confesses" to Neal that he is convinced that Gerard was a saint. Gerard's love of birds was powerful, and every act of love Gerard made was recorded in their mother's memory forever. The impact of Gerard's life and death is beyond understanding: "Neal, the death of this child was a loss that must be impossible for you and I to calculate in the souls of my mother and father" (Charters, 1995 p. 263).

These letters to Cassady continued for approximately two months and not only served as a confession for Kerouac but also were the basis of two major books he would write: *Visions of Gerard* and *Dr. Sax.* Each book is a memory of Gerard's death. Kerouac's memories illustrate the richness of affect and evolving definition of self in the context of the death and guilt that were to be his life-long preoccupations. The letters also demonstrate Kerouac's feeling that sharing these memories with Cassady would somehow change his experience of them and make them more true.

One night in 1955 Kerouac was visiting Cassady and Cassady's current girlfriend at her apartment in San Francisco. Natalie Jackson was closely associated with the group of people who frequented North Beach at that time and was known to have serious emotional problems. Cassady frequently left Kerouac alone with his girlfriends, and he did so that night. Natalie became very angry and depressed, threatening suicide. Kerouac was trying to incorporate the teachings of Buddha into his concept of Catholicism at the time, and he dealt with her feelings by explaining Buddhism to her. The actual sequence of what happened and exactly when it happened has been lost, but Natalie either fell or jumped from the roof of the apartment building to her death (Clark, 1990, pp. 141-142). Kerouac reacted by immediately leaving for his sister's home in North Carolina, where his mother was staying. However, when he arrived, his mother and sister had commitments and he was left alone. One night he had a vision of his own death and began writing down his memory of Gerard: "For the first four years of my life, while he lived, I was not Ti Jean Dulouz, I was Gerard, the world was his face, the flower of his face, The pale stopped disposition, the breakingness and the holiness and his teachings of tenderness to me" (Kerouac, 1991, p. 2).

The memory of his fusion with Gerard indicates the intensity of his identification with the figure his mother saw as a saint. The story *Visions of Gerard* contains many examples of Gerard's short, Christ-like life, his acts of love and kindness, and Kerouac's memory of his older brother as his first teacher. A new influence on Kerouac's interpretation of experience is Buddha, whom he sees as equated with Gerard in holiness. Buddha's message to Kerouac, who is terrified by the meaning of death—Gerard's, Leo's, Natalie Jackson's, and his own—is that "all is well, practice kindness, heaven is nigh!" (p. 6). In contrast to the teachings of Gerard and Buddha are the teachings of his father, who in *Visions of Gerard* tells Jack and Gerard not to worry about whether or not it was right for the cat to eat Gerard's mouse: "in life it's a jungle, man eats man either you eat or get eaten" (p. 13).

This pessimistic view of life as a Darwinian cycle to death intruded into Kerouac's seeking for spiritual comfort throughout his life. In fact, the optimistic spiritual faith of his mother, Gabrielle, and cynical pessimism of his father, Leo, are major themes in Kerouac's life. Another theme is sin, and in *Visions of Gerard* even Gerard has sins: he confesses he has pushed a boy and looked at another boy's penis in the urinal. The heavy burden of sin, original or acquired, dominates the story.

GERARD'S DEATH: OTHER MEMORIES

In *Visions of Gerard* the memory of Gerard is the one endorsed by Gabrielle and the nuns, who loved the suffering Gerard as a Christ-like figure. Kerouac does comment that in his memory he recalled not having his needs met because of the needs of Gerard, but he manages to mitigate any angry frustration by seeing how selfish his needs are compared with the needs of the suffering Gerard. He states that he knows his mother loved Gerard more than him. His life-long preoccupation with "falling from grace" begins as a four-year-old "who basked in Gerard's eternal bliss and [was] made to appreciate it as a fallen angel." An exploration of jealousy and anger as part of grief does not occur in the memory.

In his "confessional" letters to Neal Cassady, written when he was 29 years old, Kerouac explores the more puzzling and mysterious memories of Gerard. In *Visions of Gerard* he describes the erector set that Gerard received at Christmas, but it is remembered in the context of love. He watches Gerard with the set, "in the action of his hands and the working of his face as he thinks, and I marvel at my love for him" (p. 66).

To Cassady he describes the erector set in a different memory. It was just before Gerard died, and while he was working with the set the four-year-old Jack knocked part of the structure down. Gerard in "understandable rage" slapped him in the face. Even with Neal, Kerouac can remember only his guilt and sadness as a reaction to this incident, which he reports as the last thing he remembered before Gerard's death: "Gray vultures of gloomy day were feeding at the rooftops of time, I could see outside the curtains. Gloom, grayness, faucet-ticking . . ." (Charters, 1995, p. 259).

An enduring image for Kerouac throughout his life was the Great World Snake. This morbid image was intimately related to Gerard's life and death and is a metaphor of guilt and inevitable punishment. When Kerouac was three or four years old the family moved into a house that was allegedly built over an ancient, sunken cemetery. One night, lights began flashing in the bedroom. Kerouac associated this with other strange happenings in the house, such as plaster falling from the ceiling, as notification that the souls of the dead were shaking in their graves because the living had built a house on their cemetery. When Kerouac asked Gerard about the flashing lights, he replied that it was the souls of the dead. A few nights later Kerouac remembers a figure standing above his crib. Even in the letter to Cassady, Kerouac is confused as to whether it was the soon-to-be-dead Gerard risen like a ghost from his bed of miseries to haunt him or was a ghost from the disturbed cemetery. His difficulties in understanding his feelings toward Gerard are expressed to Cassady in his view that Gerard died because they lived above the cemetery, and the ghost was Gerard who "probably hated me after all."

During a time when Kerouac was aware of Gerard's impending death, he remembers believing that an evil old man haunted a house nearby. This was the

"Mighty Snake Hill Castle." This image is closely interrelated with the Dr. Sax figure and the Great World Snake that had been searching for him since he was an infant when his "sin began": "worming its way up from the middle of the world, devouring dirt, excreting dirt, inch by inch arriving, to find me in poor Lowell" (Charters, 1995, p. 250). It is unclear what he thinks his sin is. It seems vaguely related to Gerard and guilt. As an adult, Kerouac cannot say he loved Gerard simply as a person but can only describe the relationship as he remembers it as a child: admiration, love, guilt, and sadness. Gerard could be seen as a saint in *Visions of Gerard* but not more fully as a person, because of Kerouac's difficulty in exploring and understanding his own feelings of competition, jealousy, and hostility. In Kerouac's letters to Cassady, he says that Gerard's death was the beginning of his own mysteries.

Although these enduring mysteries were a source of pain for Kerouac, over time they possessed him and in the process he elevated loss and death into an ideal state. At the end of *Visions of Gerard,* Kerouac, as a small boy, sees the glory, transcendence, and joy of Gerard leaving this earth. This vision is not seen and therefore not shared by the adults. That is why they really don't understand Gerard's death and are sad.

Kerouac's sense of guilt and being a fallen angel who is the target for revengeful destruction became concretized with the fantasy of the Great Snake, which is the basis of *Dr. Sax.* However, there is no Gerard and no Catholic family morality to order experience for Kerouac in *Dr. Sax.* The image of Dr. Sax is part the cynical Leo, his father; part W. C. Fields and the con man; part the Shadow, who knows the mysteries; and part William Burroughs. The first three are memories from the past. The last, Burroughs, is a contemporary vision of an alternative route to escape the memories of the past.

A MUSE FOR THE MYSTERIES

Just before the young Jack Kerouac has his comforting vision of the true meaning of Gerard's death during his brother's funeral, he sees "the little man with the mysterious hat and then my mind swirls" (Kerouac, 1991, p. 127). Kerouac's image of the man with the mysterious hat is part of one of his most enduring and elaborate fantasies (Morrison, 1999). At the funeral, Dr. Sax is an observer of death who is associated with the more comforting conclusion about its meaning. After Gerard's death the young Kerouac had intense, often morbid "visions" and immersed himself in a series of paracosmic fantasies. One fantasy involved acting out movies with accompanying music, which developed into long serial sagas that continued for weeks. He became so involved in the roles that, recalling this as an adult, he thought the neighborhood kids knew he was crazy. These fantasies became so complicated that Kerouac wrote them as serials. Later, a playmate was killed when a milk wagon ran over him, and Kerouac saw the ghost of the boy. There was a nearby site called "the grotto" on the grounds of an orphanage that had 12 kiosk-like altars, each containing one of the 12 stations of the cross. Kerouac and his mother used to walk through the place on the way to visit his father's older brother who was fatally ill. One night, after reading the pulp magazine *The Shadow,* Kerouac was walking through the grotto and saw some kind of ghostly figure move from "station to station." This image eventually evolved into Dr. Sax. His identification with this figure was so intense that the young Kerouac began wearing a cape and going around the neighborhood at night, stealing various objects such as a pole vault and a toy wagon and frightening people by throwing tin cans through their windows.

Kerouac's models in the family for understanding death and loss did more to create anxiety and guilt than to reduce them. Gabrielle became depressed and protective of her remaining son. More intensely religious than ever, she placed cards and pictures of her favorite Catholic icon, Saint Thérése, around the house. After Gerard's death, Kerouac felt that as he walked past a picture of Saint Thérése her head turned to follow him. He witnessed his first teacher and alter ego being elevated through death to saintly status by his mother, the nuns who were his own teachers, and everyone in the neighborhood. His father lost his authority as he lost money betting on horse races, drinking, and finally losing his business. The pressure was too much, and the young Kerouac explored his fantasies for solutions.

Though an unpure hero, Dr. Sax evolved as an imaginary companion who could be an alternative to Gerard as a guide through the mysteries. Dr. Sax comes from the forest, and as a creature of the night, unlike Kerouac, is not afraid of darkness. He reduces the mystery of evil by showing that its source can be a small boy stealing a toy wagon or throwing a tin can. The image evolves over time and, in Kerouac's adulthood, Dr. Sax became a student and observer of evil whose knowledge of death and guilt made him Kerouac's "personal angel, private shadow, and secret lover" (Nicosia, 1994, p. 35).

Because Kerouac never fully explored the early images of death and loss as a child or as an adult, his understanding of them was as a child, and death remained a mystery and obsession. His teachers and models for understanding—Gerard, Gabrielle, and Leo—were themselves overwhelmed by death. Kerouac mitigated the anxiety involved by creating paracosms that he could control and understand; they served as the motivation for his first attempts as a writer. This motivation continued into adulthood and was the basis of much of his creativity. As a child Kerouac also created imaginary companions who could serve as alternatives to his family as guides: the Shadow, the Phantom, W. C. Fields, and Dr. Sax. Images and unconscious interpretations of the past will be expressed in dreams, reveries, and attempts to write about the past. But these unconscious and poorly understood memories seek expression and understanding in relationships that parallel the fantasies and serve the same motivation, which is to reduce the fear and mystery of death and loss.

WILLIAM BURROUGHS: THE HERB DIDN'T WORK

William Burroughs came from a background very different from the working-class world of Kerouac. Burroughs came from money and social status. Well read, articulate, extremely intellectual, Burroughs met Jack Kerouac at a time when Kerouac was unsure of himself and beginning to develop his creative skills as a writer. Burroughs was at Columbia University in 1944 when he met Kerouac at the apartment of Kerouac's girlfriend and eventual first wife, Edie Parker. Burroughs introduced Kerouac to people different from those he had known before. They had frequent encounters with the law, drugs, and alternative lifestyles," including homosexuality. Burroughs and Kerouac were both arrested as material witnesses in the homosexually motivated murder described earlier. Kerouac introduced Burroughs to Edie Parker's girlfriend, Joan Vollmer. Not long after Burroughs's marriage to Vollmer she was arrested and hospitalized for drug abuse. By the time Kerouac first met him, Burroughs was abusing a variety of drugs, and he was addicted most of his life. Kerouac recognized Burroughs as a major influence in his life and included him as the character Old Bull Lee in *On the Road,* and he was part of the title character in *Dr. Sax*. The childhood need to have a protector from the Great Snake, and an interpreter of death and loss that could be more comforting, found expression in childhood in Dr. Sax and in adulthood in his relationship with Burroughs.

Although Kerouac had explained his preoccupation with the Great Snake in earlier letters to Cassady, it was almost three years later, in 1962, when he was 30 years old and living with Burroughs in Mexico, that he wrote *Dr. Sax*. *Dr. Sax* is an elaborate fantasy of the preoccupation. Having externalized the source of his conflict in the fantasy of the snake, Kerouac attempts to find an external solution with the character of Dr. Sax. It is the failure of this solution in the book and in his life that is significant. At this time, Kerouac had attained little recognition as an author, was penniless, and had to leave the United States because his former wife was legally pursuing him for child support. Meanwhile, Burroughs was the subject of a criminal charge for having shot and killed his wife Joan (Vollmer) Burroughs during a game of "William Tell." The incident occurred while both were using drugs. Burroughs had an enduring preoccupation with guns and knives, and one of his favorite pastimes was target practice with his pistol. Combining his use of drugs and love of guns, he shot at benzedrine tubes placed across his room, on his farm in Louisiana (Kerouac, 1976, p. 145). Burroughs was an observer and controller of death and loss.

Kerouac had drugs with him when he arrived in Mexico. Both men used marijuana and both frequently shot up on morphine during the visit (Nicosia, 1994, p. 390; Clark, 1990, pp. 109-110). Kerouac was also experimenting with a new, nonlinear form of writing he had developed under the influence of Neal Cassady. Kerouac described this act of creativity as his mind exploding to say something about every image, every memory that would be expressed in a form beyond the confines of a story. By allowing his unconscious associations full expression, Kerouac thought he could finally get at the truth of his past. In the case of *Dr. Sax* this process is confounded by the effects of various drugs.

The book is about growing up, and events, dreams, childhood impressions, and memories are intermixed. The earliest memories are of death, and they include Gerard and a host of others: "Catholic childhood of Centraville—deaths, funerals, the shroud of that, the dark figure in the corner when you look at the deadman coffin in the dolorous parlor of the open house with a horrible purple wreath on the door" (Kerouac, 1987, p. 4). The dark figure in the corner is Dr . Sax. To reduce the anxiety and depression of this memory, Kerouac and his friends engage in sexual stimulation, masturbation, and fantasies of girls. The press of sex pushes him toward engagement, but the move toward adulthood is, in his mind, equated with the loss of a favorite toy, a ballbearing, in the mud of a neighbor's yard: "But doom came like a shot, when it did, like the foreboding said, and like implied in the laugh of Dr. Sax as he glides among the mud where my ballbearing was lost" (p. 76).

The loss of the ballbearing is significant because it was also an important part of a paracosmic game using marbles that Kerouac developed not long after Gerard's death. In this game he was able to control his chaotic, fearful experience by using marbles as race horses and handicapping them by chipping their surface. It is significant that during this time, Leo was losing control of his life by losing money on horse races. Generally, the book's mood is depressed and dominated by images such as the description in Part Four of the man with the watermelon who died on the Moody Street Bridge in the young Kerouac's presence. The one potential positive force in all of this is the character of Dr. Sax. It is the image of Dr. Sax, the Great Snake, and Kerouac's guilt and preoccupation with evil that dominate the conclusion of the book.

THE IMAGE OF DR. SAX

Probably the first articulate model of Sax is *The Phantom* radio shows and comic books that Kerouac loved when he was eight to ten years old. As an adolescent Kerouac wrote short stories of the Shadow, and the image of the dark figure and his hat, cape, and invisibility dominated his adult imagination. The Shadow was also associated with the catastrophic Lowell flood of 1936 and W. C. Fields. The consistently male figure knows what the mystery is, and although he may be a guide through the fear and anxiety, "his knowing laugh strikes terror in your heart." In a beautifully written half-dream state, in *Dr. Sax* Kerouac brings together the collected memories of Sax beginning with a scene in the alley where his father had his print shop. Multiple memories are recalled of movies seen as a child and fused with memories of real events and dreams, culminating in the flooding of the Merrimack River in 1936 and destruction of Kerouac's world. At this moment the figure of Dr. Sax, who has not yet fully appeared in the book, comes to save Kerouac. He is dressed like the Shadow and has a W. C. Fields mask. Sax has received a secret powder from a dark eagle, and Kerouac admits that they are both crazy. At this point Kerouac is writing fully in stream-of-consciousness. They explore and "know" various events in his childhood. Finally, arriving at the castle on Snake Hill where the confrontation with the Great World Snake will take place, the scene is one of judgment day. A snake as the symbol of evil rises from the pit of the castle to claim Jack: "I leaned on a stone, the Pit yawned below, I looked down to face my horror, my tormentor, mad-faced demon mirror of myself" (Kerouac, 1987, p. 238).

Dr. Sax squeezes a vial of one of his secret potions on the snake that is so powerful it causes the very earth to shake, but the snake continues to pursue Kerouac. At this point Sax is transformed again, this time to the common everyday figure who can only be William Burroughs, who says simply, "The herb didn't work."

Kerouac's morbid imagination created the symbol of guilt represented by the snake, and although the snake's wish to destroy Kerouac is externalized in the story, psychologically the self-contempt and self-loathing is internal. He seems to get closer to the internal source of his self-hatred in the conclusion of *Dr. Sax* than in any of his other published writings. The ending also reflects the failure of drugs and alcohol to enduringly reduce or modify his guilt and anxiety. Dr. Sax, in imagination, and William Burroughs, in reality, fail as guides, and the old preoccupations continue to dominate Kerouac's sense of self and view of life. Burroughs was perhaps a muse to creativity but not the guide through the mysteries that Kerouac needed. Exploring childhood memory with the aid of drugs and Dr. Sax was not the solution. Kerouac's persistence in finding an answer in a relationship resulted in what is probably his most enduring act of creativity, inspired by a muse who did not look for answers in the past.

A MUSE AT THE WHEEL: NEAL CASSADY

Kerouac's search for an idealized close male companion, the perennial lost brother, with whom he could share his thoughts and find alternatives to his own depressing conclusions about self, persisted until the latter part of his short life. The search begins with Sebastian Sampas and probably ends with Gary Snyder, the Japhy Ryder character in *The Dharma Bums.* It was approximately eight years after Gerard's death that Kerouac met Sebastian "Sammy" Sampas. The mutual admiration between the two was immediate. By all accounts Sampas was a sensitive young man who loved literature, wrote poetry, and admired Kerouac not only for his ability to write but clearly as a person. Like Kerouac, Sampas was handsome, with curly hair and a profile compared to that of Victor Mature (Amburn, 1998). Although many of their mutual friends saw Sampas either as a sissy or as feminine, and Leo referred to him as "Garbo," Kerouac referred to him in romantic terms as "a tawny lusty youth." Kerouac explored his own sexuality in his relationship with Sampas and later in life compared it to a gay love affair. Sampas was a muse who offered Kerouac the opportunity to understand his own sensuality. While he inspired Kerouac's growth as a writer, Sampas accepted the more "feminine" side of Kerouac's personality that contrasted with his other male friends, who were more typically masculine and active in sports. Sampas loved poetry and could recite it spontaneously. He motivated Kerouac to join the Young Prometheans, an intellectual group of boys who met at the Sampas home to discuss literature. Kerouac joined and began an intense relationship with Sampas. Stella, Sammy's sister, admired the young Kerouac and would later marry him. As was true of later friendships that paralleled his relationship with Sammy Sampas, Kerouac used it in his writings. Sampas under various names plays an important role in Kerouac's first novel, *The Town and the City* (published in 1950) and his later works, *Visions of Gerard* (1991), *Visions of Cody* (1993), and *Vanity of Duluoz* (1994).

Shortly after Kerouac left Lowell to enter Horace Mann in New York in preparation for Columbia University, Sampas graduated from high school and entered college to major in drama. At this time Kerouac was beginning to abuse alcohol and engage in self-destructive behavior. During Kerouac's difficult time after leaving Columbia, he shared his sense of despair with Sampas. Sampas offered to join the merchant marines and go to sea with him as a way of escaping the past. During this period Sampas expressed his deep feelings and love for Kerouac (Amburn, 1998, p. 62). At one time Kerouac considered living with Sampas. The conflicts and choices in both of their lives were brought to a head by America's entry into World War II. In 1943 Sampas joined the Army, and because of his dislike of killing he became a medic. He visited Kerouac while he was in the psychiatric unit as described earlier. In one of Sampas's last letters to his friend, he urged Kerouac to reject Western materialism and be inspired in his creativity by individualistic muses who did not look to the past for inspiration but found inspiration in new ways of looking at experiences. During his short time in the military and frequently under conditions of combat, Sampas managed to write and his work was published in *The Stars and Stripes.* He died from wounds suffered during the invasion of Anzio, Italy. From his hospital bed he requested a recorder to send a message to the boyhood friend he loved. Kerouac received the message after Sampas had died, and in the recording Sampas quotes Shelley's elegy for John Keats: "I weep for Adonais—he is dead."

Death had taken Gerard and now death took another "brother." Sampas was a different teacher. He was an explorer who was willing to commit himself to a conviction that required action. His last letter to Kerouac essentially tells his friend not to look back to Lowell and the past but to find his muse in a "noble savage " (Amburn, 1998, p. 72). In two years, death claimed another person Kerouac loved. Leo died from cancer. Soon after Kerouac met Neal Cassady, the image of the noble savage.

Kerouac first heard about Cassady from two friends who were from Denver. They had described him in legendary terms as a prodigious teenage car thief who had survived jails and reform schools since he was 14 years old. Abandoned by his mother and raised by an alcoholic father in the slums of Denver, Cassady stole cars for recreation and learned to shoot pool and hustle as a way of making money. By report he was a tremendous lover and had his first sexual encounter with a girl when he was nine years old. This legendary self-made man of action from the West also spent time studying philosophers such as Kant and Nietzsche, and writers such as Dostoyevsky and Proust. In essence Cassady had created himself against tremendous odds. The 20-year-old Cassady soon arrived in New York with his 16-year-old wife, and Kerouac made an effort to meet him.

Kerouac and his friends went to visit Cassady at his cold-water flat in Spanish Harlem. Cassady greeted them at the door completely naked, and the Kerouac contribution to the legend and myth of Neal Cassady began. The story of their relationship and travels was generated during a period of about eight years and was the basis of Kerouac's best known work, *On the Road,* and his later work, *Visions of Cody.* In the former, Cassady is Dean Moriarty, and in the latter he is Cody Pomeray. Whereas in *Visions of Gerard* Kerouac creates a memory of childhood loss modulated by a morbid French-Catholic alter ego, in *On the Road* a new way of organizing experience and understanding the past is presented through metaphors of the moving car and friendships generated through surviving shared adventures. In *Visions of Cody,* Kerouac creates the experience of Neal Cassady that is "based on my belief on the goodness of the hero and his position as an archetypical American Man" (Kerouac, 1993, introduction). Through his interpretation and creation of Neal Cassady, Kerouac thought he had found a solution to his depressive and intrusive memories. As was true of Dr. Sax, neither Dean Moriarty nor Cody Pomeray could provide enduring solutions to Kerouac's troubled view of experience. Like transitional objects, imaginary companions, a fetish, or an icon, Burroughs and Cassady served as muses and vehicles for Kerouac's needs and creative imagination. When with them, Kerouac could feel a sense of trustworthiness generated by the soothing experience of their presence, but in the light of common everyday exchange they were, finally, over time, very human.

At first Cassady enters Kerouac's life and moves him out of his depression with the force of his personality (Kerouac, 1976), and later Kerouac seeks out Cassady to escape his depression (Kerouac, 1993, Chap. 1). In both situations Kerouac is in the East in "old" New York and Cassady is the inspiration to go West to California to "find my buddy Cody again and find myself too." In the metaphors of going on the road, either with Cassady or to him, the act of movement will lead to a new view of experience and creativity, and this was the case in both *On the Road* and *Visions of Cody.* As the muse, Cassady disrupted everything as it was and "mixes up all my friends and family." For Kerouac, Cassady transformed his understanding of sex, writing, and relationships. Cassady's power comes from his personality, his example, and from Kerouac's seeing him as an heroic image of the untamed West and as a holy primitive in search of the answers to the important questions of life. Cassady was the model for creativity that Sammy Sampas had described. By action, Cassady shows that these answers won't be found in the past or in a goal. The adventures on the trip are more important than the place that was left or the destination. In fact both Kerouac and Cassady were remarkable in their need never to stay in one place. Awareness was not to be found in introspection, self-examination, or enduring relationships. Connections and satisfaction were fueled by being high and generated by movement and temporary but intense personal encounters. Cassady influenced Kerouac's use and development of the spontaneous writing style that dominates *Visions of Cody*. Using this style, memory and the unconscious became sources of creativity not because of reflective thought but because they are given unmodulated full expression. Probably Cassady's greatest source of influence on Kerouac was that Kerouac almost immediately felt that despite their differences in character, "he reminded me of some long lost brother."

Cassady is different from Gerard as teacher and guide for understanding death. Gerard was a passive, suffering victim of a powerful force. Cassady saw the power of the force, but through his own powerful skills controlling speed and motion he was in control and could challenge death. Kerouac disliked driving although he loved traveling. He had been driving a car as a teenager when he was involved in an accident. This event seems to be the point when he became phobic about driving, and he was not considered a good driver. Kerouac begins the legend of Cassady's power with speed and motion early in *On the Road* "The most fantastic parking lot attendant in the world, he can back a car forty miles an hour into a tight squeeze and stop at the wall, jump out, . . . leap into another car, circle at fifty miles an hour in a narrow space" (Kerouac, 1976, p. 9).

With Cassady (as Dean Moriarty) at the wheel, a spiritual power is guiding speed and motion away from an outcome such as death. Paraphrasing Kerouac, Cassady hunches over the wheel and guns her, propelling the companions in the car away from the confusion and nonsense of the past in the noble function of movement. Cassady's spirituality also comes from the intensity of his search and being alive to experience it. Like most saints, his answers are not always obvious to his disciples, who are often troubled by him. When he is down, and the others turn on him, Kerouac sees Cassady as "beat – the root, the soul of Beatific" and warns the others that Cassady is suffering and going mad to get the secret that they all want and need (p. 195).

The legend of Cassady becomes the myth of Cassady through his magical relationship with the car. Kerouac created this myth by simply describing Cassady as he saw him. Cassady had a spiritual bond with his car and felt he could "let his old car drive itself and it would take him where he wanted to go." Kerouac had complete faith in Cassady's ability to flirt with speeding death and then just miss it. Cassady's depth of awareness of his relationship with the car was at the level of satori and the goal was to control death: "And Dean hurled the Plymouth head-on at the truck roaring our way, wobbled and hovered in front of it a minute . . . and [would] swing away at the last moment: Like that you see, exactly like that, how bad he was" (p. 210). Riding in the car at the time, Kerouac notes that except for himself everyone else was frightened by the demonstration. He had no fear because he knew the driver was enlightened.

Later, this sharing of the spiritual experiences of death as speed and movement, in the presence of a mystical guide to the truth of the experience, is expanded upon and the psychological identity of the guide is revealed. Speeding through a storm in Colorado with two hitchhikers in the back seat, Dean continues to accelerate the car despite Sal's warnings. The car finally does spin out of control and into a ditch. Dean leaves the car to get help. "'Is he your brother?' the boys asked in the back seat. 'He's a devil with a car isn't he?—and according to his story he must be with women.' He's mad, I said, and yes, he's my brother" (p. 226).

CONCLUSION

As Kerouac described in a letter to Cassady, Gabrielle and Leo were devastated by the loss of Gerard. Kerouac's description of his experience of Gerard's death indicates that his parents could only see the lost boy as a saint. There was no one available to help the young Kerouac sort through his ambivalent feelings about his brother, and eventually the negative feelings became concretized and externalized in the enduring fantasy of the Great World Snake and the imaginary companion, Dr. Sax, as a guide through the mysteries. Kerouac never saw the Catholic saints as sources of spiritual comfort, and as a child he created Dr. Sax to reduce his sense of inadequacy while providing more comforting conclusions regarding his own "evil" than those provided by the saints of Gabrielle. His fantasy that he could be the Gerard that Gabrielle and Leo lost was not attainable. Just as J. M. Barrie's search for his brother David was a life-long preoccupation, so Kerouac's efforts to solve "the mysteries" were life-long. Like Barrie, he sought a sense of completeness in his relationships with idealized males.

Cassady, like Gerard and Sampas, died before Kerouac. When told that Cassady was dead, Kerouac simply did not believe it, and there are indications that he never accepted the loss. In some ways, Kerouac was right about Cassady being alive. Dean Moriarty and Cody Pomeroy were created by Kerouac, and that brother would always live in his imagination with Gerard and Sampas.

It is not possible to completely explain a writer's creativity by a single event such as early loss and an enduring preoccupation with death. At least four other issues contributed in various ways to Kerouac's creativity: substance abuse, sexual conflicts, maternal dependency, and spiritual confusion. Kerouac began substance abuse, particularly alcohol, early in his life. He appears to have frequently used amphetamines to get high when he wanted to write. Heavy use of amphetamines is known to cause significant neurological impairment and depression (Anglin et al., 2000). In the latter part of his life, Kerouac was clearly an alcoholic, as he described himself in *Big Sur.* Another major issue in Kerouac's life was his difficulty with his sexuality. During his most creative period two of his closest friends, Alan Ginsberg and Burroughs, were definitely homosexual, and Cassady could enter into a sexual relationship with either men or women depending on his needs at the time. It would appear that Kerouac had strong homosexual desires that he had a difficult time accepting (Amburn, 1998).

Finally, there are the related issues of his relationship with his mother and his search for religious faith. Although Kerouac's life was one of moving from one place to another, the pattern was that he always returned to his mother. He was extremely dependent on Gabrielle, and there are indications that she never approved of his friends or his lifestyle. Throughout her life she was a Catholic woman of traditional values who had strong negative feelings about Jews and homosexuals (Nicosia, 1994). Kerouac died an alcoholic at the age of 47. Stella Sampas (his wife and the sister of his close boyhood friend, Sammy) and Gabrielle were there. One of the most enduring qualities of this writer of loss was the wish to have a mother, or mother figure, take care of him, as he consistently did not take care of himself.

Gabrielle had taken care of Gerard, who was clearly worthy of her care. In the latter part of his life, as Kerouac constantly sought the companionship and care of his mother; he lived a life she could not approve of as he sank deeper into spiritual bankruptcy. He tried to escape his Catholic faith and guilt by following Buddhism. The attempt was a failure, and he later admitted that the teachings of Buddha had escaped him. The reason may be found here: "I see there in the eyes of Gerard the very diamond kindness and patient humanity of the Brotherhood Ideal propounded from afar down the eternal corridors of Buddahood" (Kerouac, 1991, p. 7). In a religion that stresses transformation of inner states rather than images of the saints and God to concretize the spiritual goal, Kerouac's memory and imagination fill his own spiritual void with the image of Gerard's eyes: ". . . and immortal idealism which had been imparted to me by my holy brother" (p. 6). The spiritual teachings of Buddha and the presence of the Holy Spirit in the icons of Catholic faith are powerfully fused by a memory of an idealized lost brother, as understood by a child.

CHAPTER 10

Final Thoughts: Loss, Love, and Creativity

It is to a poet a thing of awe
to find that history is true.
Isak Dinesen, *The River*

As we stated in the Introduction, this book is a study of the development of imagination in childhood and the effects on this development of the early loss of a psychologically important family member and unsuccessful grieving. For the child, unsuccessful grieving is the result of anxiety and unresolved conflicts related to the lost family member, who is now the object not of ongoing experience but of compensatory memory. As the child becomes conscious of these unacceptable wishes toward the deceased, internal anxiety is generated. Repression of these wishes reduces the anxiety, and the unconscious develops. The major defense is identification with the idealized lost sibling or parent. This happens at a time in development when differentiation of self and recognition of the independence of others is in progress. Because of issues related to development, the consequences of unsuccessful grieving are unique in children, and loss and unsuccessful grieving in children are quite different from these experiences in adults (Anderson, 1949; Malinak, Hoyt, & Patterson, 1979). Children experience major disruptions in the development of representational, reflective, and autonomous thought. This profoundly affects the child's developing awareness of self and the capacity to be aware of the psychological states of others. The enduring effects of the conflicts of unsuccessful grieving formed in childhood can be seen in the adult whose preoccupations with death and loss lead to chronic feelings of low self-esteem, depression, and a sense of incompleteness. This results in repeated efforts by the adult to enter into romanticized relationships that serve to temporarily reduce their feelings of low self-esteem and to mitigate the painful memories of the past. Imagination is both restricted and enriched by the intensity of the emotions and memories of loss. For some individuals these painful memories result in creative stories that explore the past and construct a contemporary conclusion that is more supportive of their wished for relationships and fantasies about self. Successful grieving in children takes time and is less complicated when the lost individual is loved and not the object of ambivalent or strong negative feelings that are difficult for the child to explore consciously.

To understand this psychological process of loss and grief, the focus of this text has been on a child's inner experience of loss and the consequent effect on imagination. The family's contribution to the child's experience of the loss of a family member is in itself a subject for an entire book (Walsh & McGoldrick, 1991). Here we examine some of the issues regarding the effect of the family on a child's experience of loss and the development of imagination and creativity.

LOSS, LOVE, IMAGINATION, AND THE FAMILY

As we have noted, it is in the context of the family that the child learns about love, with the emotional intensity of the first experience of attachment and intimacy. The child's level of cognitive and emotional development, as well as the circumstances of a death and loss, will contribute to the child's reaction to the trauma and stress inherent in the event. These factors interact with the family structures to determine the outcome of the grieving process. The child's initial reaction to the loss of a parent or sibling includes normal emotional and psychophysical responses as well as confusion as he or she attempts to understand this profound event that affects the whole family. This may contribute to a feeling of being alone and isolated from the more mature and older members of the family. The family's attention is with the deceased, not the child. This may result in the child's conclusion that he or she is not as emotionally important to the family as was the lost family member.

Both J. M. Barrie (1901) and Jack Kerouac (1991) wrote about their experience of the loss of a brother and the family's reaction that contributed to their understanding of loss and grief. The grieving parents in a family have the burden of dealing with their own feelings as well as being aware of the feelings of the remaining family members. As children, both Barrie and Kerouac felt that they were not as important to their mothers as was the lost older brother, and both tried to become the lost son for their grieving and depressed mother. This was also true of Tyrone, in our case story, in his relationship with his mother, Vernez. Rather than sharing their grief with their sons and helping them come to terms with what the loss meant to them, the mothers made what could have been a mutual grieving process an experience that was essentially their own. Consequently, the children's understanding of loss was confounded in important psychological ways with the needs of their mothers. Paradoxically for Tyrone, Barrie, and Kerouac, the sense of not belonging or being unimportant in the family was mitigated by the fantasy that they could gain status and importance by becoming the idealized lost son.

The death of a sibling or a parent has lifelong implications for the surviving child. Such children need a parent who is available to help them express the full range of their feelings in a supportive, understanding relationship. In these situations the child's feelings are validated through exploration, understanding, and eventual ownership. Under these emotional and interpersonal conditions, the children feel that they have been comforted, taught, and included as individuals in the family experiences. They have a sense that they know more about themselves, the lost family member, and their own relationships in the family. Successful grieving has been accomplished, and the child's access to imagination and affect can continue along a normal developmental course. Where a child's experience and understanding of death and loss is incongruous with that of the other family members, and this psychological state is unresolved, unsuccessful grieving occurs and endures. The development of the child's imagination and memory becomes over-determined by preoccupations with how fragile love is when death intrudes.

CONFLICT, IMAGINATION, AND CREATIVITY IN CHILDHOOD

The importance of a supportive family environment that accepts the child as an individual and encourages his or her creative talents is widely acknowledged (Singer & Singer, 1990). At the same time, there is a known relationship between unstable and conflicted family experiences in childhood and later creativity (Albert, 1978) as well as evidence suggesting that the early loss of a parent or sibling in childhood is related to later adult creativity (Pollack, 1962, 1978; Schultz, 1996). It is also clear, however, that a childhood in a chaotic and stressed family or the experience of early loss does not necessarily result in adult creativity or an adult life of psychopathology or crime and violence. Actually, as illustrated by the four authors considered in this text, creative adults who have experienced early loss often are not content with who they are, are often depressed, and seldom find enduring satisfaction in relationships. Obviously, creativity in adults can be related to experiences in childhood other than early loss. For the child there may be a number of intense early memories—such as the moment a father cried after losing his business, or times the mother expressed intense anger for something the child said—that generate troublesome questions. For the sensitive child, such moments motivate a life-long exploration for answers. The early loss of a parent or sibling could be a source of these troublesome questions. In a circumstance that is unique to childhood, the memory of the event is an interaction between the child's intense emotional experiences and a poorly articulated conclusion of self that is a function of both the experience and the child's egocentric projections.

The model used in this text for understanding the relationship between creativity and these memories of early loss is the importance of repression and compensatory identification with the lost parent or sibling that creates a vacuum in memory, resulting in the need to master the early experience of self and answer the troublesome questions. The understanding of these past events is formed prior to the development of stable cognitive structures and socialized thoughts. Because of anxiety, access to these repressed experiences of self is limited, and efforts to explore their meaning result in creative expressions that are unique to the child and later the adult. For the child who has experienced early loss and unsuccessful grieving, the images and symbols of this memory produce anxiety and are intense, idiosyncratic, and restricted in content. As seen in the play of both Benny and Tyrone in our case stories, these internal images and symbols may be expressed in the metaphors of play. The compulsion to know the past and self is always confounded by being represented by images and symbols that simultaneously suggest a truth and create confusion. The relationship between these representations of the past, psychopathology, and creativity is complex.

FIRST REPRESENTATIONS AND CREATIVITY

Access to what Freud (1923) described as primary process and Piaget (1962) called preoperational thought has been considered a source for creative expression (Russ, 1993; Singer & Singer, 1990). The importance for creativity of primary process and preoperational thought is that both influence the child's first understanding of experience before development of more integrated and coherent cognitive structures, and both are characterized by the dominance of affective states in their organization. The theoretical interrelationship of primary process thought and preoperational thought has been the subject of considerable study. For the development of imagination, the important issue is the nature of the child's first representations of experiences prior to the development of secondary thought in Freudian theory, or operational thought in Piaget's theory. The idiosyncratic images and symbols generated during this period have major influences on the articulation and differentiation of both affect and imagination. Examples of current views of how primary thought relates to the child's accommodation to experience through the use of secondary process are found in Fast (1985) and Noy (1979). Examples of the relationship between preoperational thought and operational thought are found in Flavell (1963), and the relationship between preoperational thought and childhood imagination are described by Fraiberg (1959). Greenspan (1979) provides a well-thought-out discussion of the relationship between the contemporary theories of Freud and Piaget.

The child's first ways of representing and analyzing experiences are characterized by internally generated aggressive and libidinal content and formal processes such as illogical thinking, fusion of ideas, and images with loose associative links. Representations of external events are formed by the child's perceptions and idiosyncratic symbols that are not a function of logical constructs or socialized thought. Representations are structured by realism, animism, and artificialism and are organized prior to the differentiation of self and reflective thought (Piaget, 1962). If repression occurs for these first representations of experience, they become unconscious and are not modified by accommodations to the child's later experience. At about age two, the child begins to develop more stable cognitive structures that evolve over time into socialized representations, consistent use of reflective thought, and eventually autonomous representations of self and experience. The unconscious will disrupt this development.

Conscious access to these original ways of thinking has been the subject of considerable research. A good deal of this research has evolved from the Holt (1977) scoring system for primary process responses on the Rorschach projective test (Rorschach, 1942). Originally developed for use with adults, the system has a variety of scoring categories, but the Adaptive Regression (AR) score has proved to have a consistent relationship to creativity in adults. The AR score measures the intensity of primary process material and a subject's cognitive ability to integrate this material. Using various criteria of creativity, the AR score has been shown to relate to problem-solving efficiency, divergent thinking, and a number of other indications of adult creativity (Russ, 1993). Holt's scoring system has also been used to study creativity in children. The Primary Process (PP) score, a measure of what has been defined as pure access to primary process material and the adaptiveness of the responses, has proved useful with children. For example, compared with a lower-scoring group, children scoring high on a formal test of creative thinking demonstrated more total primary process ideation on the Rorschach, as well as effective use of regression (Dudek & Verreault, 1989). Using second-graders and controlling for the effects of intelligence, Russ (1980) found a significant relationship between AR scores and reading achievement. Boys' scores on AR were significantly related to the ability to change an old set of problem-solving skills for a new one that could solve a new task requiring a shift in hypothesis. This divergent thinking and transformation ability and adaptive regression capacity was found in boys and not girls. In a summary of series of studies using the AP and PP scores, Russ (1993) found that controlled access to primary process thinking and creativity occurs with boys but not girls. This consistent gender difference in the Holt scoring system and childhood creativity is a methodological issue and suggests that the Holt scoring system may not be appropriate as an indicator of primary process and creativity in girls. The research results with boys is consistent. Rorschach responses indicating adaptive access to primary process are related to the ability to shift problem-solving strategies, divergent thinking, and artistic creativity. In boys, the capacity to access primary process thinking is related to cognitive components found in creative thought.

PLAY AND CREATIVITY

These first representations of childhood experience found in the images and affects of primary process on projective tests are also expressed in a child's play, and there is an association between particular components of play and childhood creativity. Play serves a number of functions in childhood. In terms of play and creativity, play combines imagination, affect, and adaptive cognitive processes in unique ways. Although fantasy is dominant, play stimulates the formation of images that are stored in memory to be used in integrated combinations in play activities reflecting both fantasies and experience. Play encourages creative imagery of the past while providing the opportunity to anticipate a more realistic future. The capacity for imaginative play contributes to the development of language and strategies for problem solving, as well as divergent thinking. When play is shared with other children, social skills develop (Russ, 1993; Singer & Singer, 1990). The contribution of the affective components of play to cognitive development and creativity has only recently been a subject of research. The child's ability to express both positive and negative feeling and thoughts in imaginative play, without the intrusion of anxiety, is important for the continuity of both individual and social play. The expression of feeling states and interpersonal emotions in play allows the child to experience them in the relatively safe confines of pretend. In this context, children may gain a capacity to reflect on their experience and use their emotions creatively. Threatening thoughts that could not be expressed because of anxiety can find expression and elaboration in play. Under the safe condition of pretend, the child can use cognitive strategies to understand and modulate affective material.

In this view of play, access to primary thought and exploration of its meaning result in the modification of primary processes through the development and integration of secondary processes. Play activities and fantasies organized by preoperational thought are modified by the use of various cognitive strategies seen in operational thought. As the child matures, play reflects the affective and cognitive integration of the different ways of thinking as modulated by an awareness of self (Pine, 1985, Chap. 5). In either theoretical model, access to original ways of organizing experience and capacity to express and integrate affective content in pretend play are considered an important component in the child's ability to think creatively.

The study of the relationship between affect expressed in play and creativity has been advanced by the development of the Affect in Play scales (Russ, 1993, Chap. 4). The scales are appropriate for a child from five to ten years of age. The procedure is individually administered and samples the child's play with two puppets for five minutes. The goal of the procedures is to measure the amount and types of affective expression and cognitive dimensions, such as quality of fantasy and imagination. Based on affective scales developed by Holt (1977) for primary process on the Rorschach, and on play scales developed by Singer (1973), the Affect in Play scales provide a quantified system for scoring three dimensions of affect in fantasy: 1) affect experienced through expression of feeling states; 2) affective content, including primary process themes such as oral aggression and anal fantasies; 3) cognitive integration of affect reflecting the combination of quality-of-fantasy scores and affect scores. The scoring system has demonstrated reliability in two studies using first- and second-graders. The scales have been used to establish a significant relationship between the frequency of primary process thought in the child's responses to the Rorschach and the following activities in play with the two puppets: frequency of both primary and non-primary affect, variety of affect, comfort with affective expression, and quality of fantasy and imagination. These relationships between PP scores on the Rorschach and the Affect in Play scales occurred for boys and girls. In a study of affect and creativity, affect displayed in play was consistently related to a child's performance on an alternative use test. A factor analysis of the Affect in Play scales established a dominant cognitive factor that included four major scales of imagination, organization, quality of fantasy, and comfort in play. A second factor clustered around the scales for affective expression and included frequency of affective responses and the scales for intensity of affect and variety of affective categories. The results indicate that the Affect in Play scale is measuring two separate processes—affective expression and cognitive control—that occur during a child's play, but they can be considered related yet independent processes.

SOURCES OF CREATIVITY IN CHILDHOOD

A major emphasis in this text has been the importance of the child's first ways of cognitively organizing experience. These representations are affect-laden, organized before development of the stable controls of later cognitive systems, and are idiosyncratic and egocentric. These affective-cognitive systems continue to influence the child's interpretation and memory of experience for a considerable time, but gradually are significantly modified by positive interpersonal experiences that contribute to reflective thought and eventually autonomous thought. If the positive interpersonal process occurs, affect and cognition are integrated, and the child's capacity for reciprocal, affective expression and love in relationships can develop. This individual is relatively free of conflicts and can think autonomously. He or she is capable of the divergent thinking that is important in scientific work and may be exceptionally creative in such endeavors (Feist, 1991). Development of the capacity for reflective and autonomous thought is disrupted when the child experiences loss and unsuccessful grieving. This results in four major interrelated psychological processes that influence the child's imagination: 1) development of internal anxiety and repression of related conflicted ideation, 2) compensatory unconscious identification with the idealized deceased family member, 3) chronic preoccupation with the meaning of loss, and 4) an enduring motivation to create a different story of the event. Creativity is motivated by the wish to address these troublesome issues and is enriched by the intrusive first representations of this experience that have been used to understand the event. Any focused, stressful event in the child's early experiences that has resulted in the development of repression to reduce anxiety related to ideation that has not been adequately understood, and not adequately integrated by reflective thought, will have the same or similar psychological outcome. The stressful event always involves the child's evolving understanding of self and others. The significant issue is that autonomous thought is compromised. A major difference between creativity in the domain of science and creativity in the domain of art and literature is that the unconscious affect-laden memories of the past compromise autonomous thought while enriching the understanding of experiences.

The focus of the research on the relationship between access to primary process thinking and creativity has been on children who generally did not share the history of the children who are the focus of this text (Dudek & Verreault, 1989; Russ, 1993). The imagination of these child research subjects was monitored by autonomous thought. Pervasive, intrusive, and egocentric first representation of experience can also be a source of creativity. The relationship between a history of psychological difficulties and creativity in adulthood has been the subject of considerable research (Runco & Richards, 1997). Creativity has been associated with mood disorders, alcoholism, schizophrenia, and manic-depression disorder. Psychometric studies have found deviant, antisocial, and abrasive traits in creative adults, and there is evidence of shared cognitive styles in creative and schizophrenic adults. The study of pathological conditions and creativity in adults has demonstrated a diverse basis for creativity. It indicates that the source of creative thought is not limited to those who have conscious access to affective states and primary process thought modulated by autonomous thought, but may also be found in individuals who are chronically, or at times, dominated by these affective and cognitive conditions with a related significant compromise in autonomous thought.

As seems to be true of such adults who are creative, the child who has experienced unsuccessful grieving may not always have conscious access to primary process thought, but the experience of these early affect-laden memories may intrude into and find expression in his or her consciousness. The study of such children could add to our understanding of the contribution to creativity of conflicts generated by the first ways of thinking. For these children, access to primary process and creativity may vary with content and affect. For example, using a modification of the Holt (1977) scoring system, the PP, AR, and Defense Effectiveness scores of Rorschach responses of children with a history of unsuccessful grieving may demonstrate systematic variation. Comparison with an appropriate control group may demonstrate that a child's responses to the Rorschach that reflect the effects of loss and depression may result in lower AR scores, while other responses that are not subject to ideation related to loss may be in the expected range. Content analysis of the individual child's protocol may indicate the source of the variation in cognitive control. Another possibility is that responses to particular Rorschach cards that stimulate depressive content may reflect the child's preoccupation with death and loss with scores that are high on defensive demand, indicating intensity of content. In another child's protocol the responses may demonstrate high defense effectiveness, suggesting that affect is adequately expressed and integrated in the response. This child may be demonstrating progress in grieving, whereas a child demonstrating an opposite pattern of scores may be conflicted. Application of the Holt system may demonstrate particular patterns of scores reflecting the individual child's progress in grieving and may provide data for establishing subgroups that show different levels and perhaps patterns of conscious access to primary process thought with related uses of imagination.

The relationships between a child's progress in grieving, imagination, and creativity as indicated by PP scores on the Rorschach, or any projective techniques, will be complex. For example, it is not clear whether a typical test of creativity used in previous research on primary process thinking and creativity, such as a reading test or a test of flexibility-rigidity, would be a relevant measure of creativity in this group. Any procedure that measures the more cognitive aspects of creativity without an adequate procedure for measuring the child's affect and interpersonal reactions would not be appropriate. Representations of unsuccessful grieving would contain morbid imagery and anxiety with poor organization, because of inadequate reflective thought for this content. Creative, original images with unique metaphors of loss and recovery may occur in the child whose representations of past experiences are less anxiety-laden. An appropriate measure of creativity may be obtained in activities that enable the child to express the representation of the past in play, drawing, story telling, drama, and dance, or a combination of any of these activities. Quantification of creativity may focus on the occurrence of metaphor and novel imagery, the originality and sequence in the stories told, as well as the psychological meaning in the story content and ending. Pretend play involving imaginary playmates and complex paracosms may indicate the child's adaptive reaction to loss by integrating fantasy and creative imagination for positive conclusion. The development of character and emotional support in relationships indicate the socialization process and should be noted.

These modalities for the expression of adaptive imagination and creativity may be used as independent measures of creative expression, providing construct validity for other relevant quantified observations. For example, a child's PP scores on the Rorschach and the Affect in Play scales (Russ, 1993) could be compared with the child's creative capacity to tell stories or express fantasy in art. Alternative theoretical orientation could prove useful. For example, scoring systems that reflect a Piagetian view, such as those developed using Event Theory, could be used with the Rorschach, as well as activities that demonstrate cognitive-emotional differentiation and integration (Fast, 1985). Issues such as age appropriateness and systems of quantification would have to be addressed.

It is significant that, as children, the four authors of loss discussed in this text devoted considerable time to the elaboration of imaginary worlds. The Brontë children, Emily, Branwell, Charlotte, and Anne, all participated in creation of the paracosm of Glasstown. Not long after the death of David, J. M. Barrie and his mother began to write the story of a young girl's world that eventually resulted in Wendy and Neverland. Jack Kerouac created inner, silent movies in which he portrayed all the characters. These movies became long serial sagas that Kerouac, as an adult, saw as his first creative efforts—efforts that began soon after the death of Gerard. The adult Kerouac saw these fantasies as indications that he might be going crazy. By age eight, Isak Dinesen had demonstrated obvious talent in writing prose and poetry. She also illustrated many of her stories. It would appear, then, that as children these writers had a talent for narrative expression and imaginary reconstruction of experience that was stimulated by the troublesome questions generated by the experience of loss. This resulted in stories from childhood on that were characterized by an in-depth involvement in a poorly understood memory and affect-laden images that became a major way of understanding the past, experiencing the present, and anticipating the future. With a restricted development of reflective thought and insight, this cognitive set was reinforced and nurtured by the individuals' experiences, which resulted in an understanding that was a fusion of the actual event and the individual's limited access to conscious thought.

Assimilation always dominated accommodation. Emily Brontë experienced the loss of Branwell, and created the romance of Heathcliff and Catherine. J. M. Barrie experienced with his mother the loss of his brother, and told the story in the metaphors of the romance of Tommy and Grizel and Peter and Wendy. Loving and losing an idealized, powerful, and self-destructive father, Isak Dinesen later told of the experience of love and tragic loss in the death of an equally powerful man, Denys Finch-Hatton. Jack Kerouac's childlike memories of loss generated by Gerard's death found full and powerful expression in *Dr. Sax* and *Visions of Gerard*. The examples of childhood creativity in the four authors suggest how children use the experience of loss to create and indicate a focus for future research. The examples also illustrate the importance of observing the child's family relationships that may have a positive or negative effect on imagination and creativity. It seems clear that in each case, the ability to create was stimulated by important relationships in the family: the close emotional ties of the Brontë children, the almost symbiotic relationship of Barrie and his mother, the sense of isolation that Dinesen felt with her mother and sisters, and Kerouac's sense of sin in the context of his mother's strong religious beliefs. Research on imagination and creativity must include the relationships of the creative person. It is a mistake to see imagination and creativity as an essentially internal process of the individual. In both children and adults, creativity is often significantly influenced by relationships. For the creative adult this can be collaborative efforts in science and the arts (John-Steiner, 2000), or it may be based on the emotional relationship of the romance with a muse, as discussed in this text.

FIRST MEMORIES AND ADULT CREATIVITY

Guided by theory, we have used the case study method to trace the sources and expression of imagination and creativity (Gruber 1988). In terms of the unique issues related to imagination, early loss, and unsuccessful grieving in children, this is a legitimate approach. Lacking the controls available in a group design with creativity as a manipulated variable, the interpretation and generalizations of the findings in the case study method are limited. Whether an imaginative child, or a group of children, with a specific characteristic or a particular history will eventually be found to be creative as an adult is probably a function of the interaction of events over time (Feldman, 1999). These include the individual's cognitive strengths relative to the domain, the social-emotional experience within and outside the family, educational and learning experience, opportunities to practice a skill in the domain, and, as the child matures into an adult, the relevance of the individual's creative skills to the state of the field at the time. The focus of this approach is less on the study of an exceptional individual, and that person's known achievement in a domain, than on the development of the person in a social context that includes broad, historical patterns that constrain and select particular creative individuals. Although this approach highlights the possible multiple influences on the development of creativity, it also illustrates some of the major methodological issues that would have to be addressed in a longitudinal study. The prediction performance issues in such a longitudinal study are considerable (Morrison & Mantzicopoulos, 1990).

Another approach is to interview creative adults, such as painters and authors, who have some eminence in their field, focusing on their early histories. The history interview would include life events that are considered theoretically significant in the development of creativity. To avoid the possible conscious and unconscious motives that may systematically affect memory, the interviews could include a story completion task. The Narrative Completion Test (NCT) was developed to obtain systematically the details of an individual's history and early experience. The procedure is self-administered and has questions about different characters in situations relevant to self-evaluation and interpersonal motivation. Stories also include content such as dreaming and association with early memories at different age ranges (Segal et al., 2001-2002). The NCT is a story completion task that has a stem that precedes to the situation description, which prompts participants to create narratives that include events, feelings, and psychological experiences. The procedure has had limited application, but results indicate that adults who saw their childhood as undesirable were currently depressed and had negative memories of their mother. The NCT scores obtained from 171 undergraduate students between 18 and 21 years of age were used for a convergent analysis. This statistical procedure showed that the NCT does measure memories of early life events that influence the stories told by this sample of college students. The developers of the NCT interpret this result as indicating that memories of childhood events are the earliest influence on the way an individual tells a story. Although this may be true to some degree, the actual association with early childhood memories, creating stories, and independent indications of adult creativity, has yet to be demonstrated with the NCT. As the developers of the NCT suggest, the procedure needs to be used with a wider range of subjects. Used with a group of published authors of fiction it might be a productive procedure for demonstrating possible associations between various aspects of childhood experience and the content of the authors' stories. It would have been interesting to examine the NCT protocols of Brontë, Barrie, Dinesen, and Kerouac.

Beyond the specific effect on imagination of the memory of early loss and unsuccessful grieving is the general issue of memories of childhood experiences and adult imagination. The first ways of knowing that dominate the child's organization of experience from the first representations to the establishment of reflective thought, roughly from age two to middle childhood, form memories that can never be created again after the formation of more mature cognitive structures. These are psychologically the magic years (Fraiberg, 1959). Cognitive development and social experience modify these original memories, but these early modes of knowing continue to influence adult assimilation of and accommodation to later experience. In the normal course of development and experience, the adult continues to be in touch with these affects and ways of knowing in ways that enrich individual and interpersonal experience. Such adults can appreciate the arts and may contribute to the domain of their choice. They most often show curiosity and what might be called a childlike quality in their enthusiasm for novelty. If they are involved in creative efforts, they demonstrate as much cognitive investment in the process of creation as they do in the end product. They often have an intense emotional involvement in their work and are frequently disappointed, as well as delighted and surprised when the outcome matches their creative goal. They appreciate the creativity of others and are invested in their own creative efforts. Whether or not their efforts gain any level of social acceptance is a complicated issue involving multiple individual and social factors.

The effort to understand the development of imagination and creativity in this text has been based on the examination of the child and of the adult who, as a child, experienced a tragic event with the result that a need for mastery resulted in creativity. Tyrone's depression was briefly lessened by his rich fantasy of the magical basketball game with his imagined dead brother. The content of the game, and the transference to the therapist, was based on the tragic death of Lucas.

The four authors of loss found creativity in loss, and their lives as adults were characterized by periods of relative happiness when they were involved in the creative process with individuals who stimulated their imagination. Enduring periods of satisfaction and happiness did not seem to be a major theme in their stories or their lives. No claim is made here that such histories in childhood are a major source of the motivation to create. The childhoods of adults who are later seen as creative are varied, and no one pattern of early experience can adequately account for later creativity (Feldman, 1999). The personality of the creative adult has been the subject of extensive study, with the general conclusion that creative individuals do not have a single trait but demonstrate a wide range of personality characteristics. Existing data suggest that the explanation of the path from imagination in childhood to the eventual expression of creativity in any domain will not be found in a simple paradigm.

THE PLEASURE IN FANTASY

Imagination is limitless and not bound by the restraints and demands of application within the limitations of external experience. As fanciful as the individual wants to be with no limitations, the fantasies formed in imagination, when modified by the restraint of reality, can result in creative conclusions. Early childhood representations of the past are characterized by satisfying fantasies and pretend play that existed in an egocentric, cognitive state. The modification of that state by social experience is a continual process that does not remove that early way of thinking from conscious expression. These original ways of thinking can be expressed again in adulthood when more social ways of experience are suspended. This occurs frequently and is a major source of adult satisfaction (Singer & Singer, 1990; Vanderberg, 1991). The normal adolescent in romantic love demonstrates the capacity to understand the sources of love in both current and future relationships as a combination of fantasy, projection, and idealized states. Many movies are created with the assumption that the adult viewer will willingly suspend belief and engage in a fantasy that does not correspond to the reality immediately outside the door of the theater. On a larger scale, society recognizes the need of the adult to engage with other adults in games of pretend that allow individuals to be someone or something else at a different time and place. Examples include large-scale enactments of various Civil War battles and the annual Mardi Gras activities in New Orleans and other cities.

The wish for a different experience from everyday existence is stimulated by memories formed at a time in childhood when events were experienced and structured by imagination and fantasy motivated by wish. Some creative individuals have recognized their capacity to go back to that time and consciously use those images as a source of their creativity. Almost two hundred years ago, a poet was feeling that he lacked inspiration. His work was tedious and "disowned by memory." He thought there was a solution to this lack of inspiration:

> Meanwhile, my hope has been that I might fetch
> Invigorating thoughts from former years,
> Might fix the wavering balance of my mind. . . .
>
> Of visionary things, and lovely forms
> And sweet sensations that throw back our life
> And almost make our infancy itself
> A visible scene, on which the sun is shining. . . .
>
> William Wordsworth, *The Prelude* (1805)

Bibliography

Albert, R. S. (1971). Cognitive development and parental loss among the gifted and creative. *Psychological Reports, 29,* 19-26.

Albert, R. S. (1978). Observations and suggestions regarding gifted, familial influence, and the achievement of eminence. *Gifted Child Quarterly, 22,* 201-211.

Amburn, E. (1998). *Subterranean Kerouac.* New York: St. Martins Press.

Anderson, C. (1949) Aspects of psychological grief and mourning. *International Journal of Psychoanalysis, 30,* 48-55.

Anglin, M., Burke, C., Perrochet, B., Stamper, E., & Dawnd-Noursi, S. (2000). History of Mathanphetamine problem. *Journal of Psychoactive Drugs, 32*(2), 137-141.

Asquith, C. (1954) *Portrait of Barrie.* London: James Barrie.

Baldwin, A. L. (1967) *Theories of child development.* New York: John Wiley.

Barren-Cohen, S. (1991) Do people with autism understand what causes emotions? *Child Development, 62,* 385-395.

Barrie, J. M. (1901). *The novels, tales, and sketches of J. M. Barrie, Vol. III: Margaret Ogilvy.* New York: Charles Scribner's Sons.

Barrie, J. M. (1902). *The little white bird or adventures in Kensignton Gardens.* New York: Charles Scribner's Sons.

Barrie, J. M. (1964). *Peter Pan.* London: Penguin Books.

Barrie, J. M. (1911). *Peter and Wendy.* London: Hodder and Stoughton.

Barrie, J. M. (1943). *Tommy and Grizel.* New York: The Press of the Readers Club.

Bellak, L., & Bellak, S. (1950). An introductory note on the child's aperception test (CAT). *Journal of Projective Techniques, 14,* 173-180.

Bently, P. (1969). *The Brontës and their world.* London: Thames and Hudson.

Birkin, A. (1979). *J. M. Barrie & the lost boys.* New York: Clarkson N. Potler.

Bowlby, J. (1960). Grief and mourning in infancy and early childhood. *Psychoanalytical Study of the Child, 15,* 9-22.

Bowlby, J. (1969) *Attachment.* New York: Basic Books.

Brontë, E. (1960). *Wuthering Heights.* New York: Holdt, Rinehard & Winston.

Butterworth, G. E., Harris, P., Leslie, A., & Wellman, H. M. (1991). *Perspectives on the child's theory of the mind.* Oxford: Oxford University Press.

Cain, C., Fast, I., & Erickson, M. (1964). Children's disturbed reaction to the death of a sibling. *American Journal of Orthopsychiatry, 34*(4), 741-752.

Charters, A. (1995). *Jack Kerouac: Selected letters.* New York: Viking.

Clark, T. (1990). *Jack Kerouac*. New York: Paragon House.

Cohen, D., & Mackeith, S. (1991). *The development of imagination*. New York: Routledge.

Cohen, J., Mannarino, A., Greenberg, T., Padlo, S., & Shipley, C. (2002). Childhood traumatic grief. *Trauma, Violence, and Abuse, 3*(4), 307-327.

Dinesen, I. (1934). *Seven Gothic tales*: New York: Modern Library.

Dinesen, I. (1937). *Out of Africa*. New York: Modern Library.

Dinesen, I. (1957). *Last tales*. New York: Random House.

Dinesen, I. (1981). *Letters from Africa* (1914-1931). Chicago: University of Chicago Press.

Dinesen, I. (1993). *Winter's tales*. New York: Vintage Books.

Dudek, S., & Verreault, R. (1989). The creative thinking and ego functioning of children. *Creativity Research Journal, 2*, 64-86.

Fast, I. (1985) *Event theory*. Hillsdale, NJ: Lawrence Erlbaum.

Feist, G. J. (1991) Synthetic and analytic thought: Similarities among art and science students. *Creativity Research Journal, 4*, 145-155.

Feldman, D. H. (1999). The development of creativity. In R. J. Sternberg (Ed.), *Handbook of creativity*. New York: Cambridge University Press.

Flavell, J. H. (1963). *The developmental psychology of Jean Piaget*. New York: Van Nostrand.

Fonagy, P. (1989). On toleration mental states: Theory of mind in borderline personality. *Bulletin of the Anne Freud Center, 12*, 91-115.

Fonagy, P., & Moran, G. S. (1991). Understanding psychic change in child analysis. *International Journal of Psychoanalysis, 72*, 15-22.

Fraiberg, S. (1959) *The magic years*. New York: Scribners.

Fraser, R. (1988). *The Brontës*. New York: Fawcett Columbine.

Freidlander, S., & Morrison, D. (1980), Childhood. In K. Pope (Ed.), *On love and loving*. San Francisco: Jossey-Bass.

Freud, S. (1923). *The ego and the id. Standard Edition, 19*, 21-66. London: Horgarth Press.

Freud, S. (1961). *Beyond the pleasure principle*. New York: Norton.

Gardner, H. (1983). *Frames of mind*. New York: Basic Books.

Gérin, W. (1971). *Emily Brontë*. Oxford: Clarendon Press.

Gopnik, A., & Meltzoff, A. (1998). *Words, thoughts and theories*. Cambridge, MA: MIT Press.

Greenspan, S. I. (1979). *Intelligence and adaptation*. New York: International Universities Press.

Gruber, H. (1988). The evolving systems approach to creative work. *Creativity Research Journal, 1*, 27-51.

Hammer, E. (1980) *The clinical application of projective drawings*. Springfield, IL: Charles C. Thomas.

Hatfield, C. W. (Ed.). (1941). *The complete poems of Emily Jane Brontë*. New York: Columbia University Press.

Holt, R. R. (1977). A method for assessing primary process manifestation and their control in Rorschach responses. In Rickers-Ovsiankina (Ed.), *Rorschach psychology*. New York: Krieger Publisher.

John-Steiner, V. (2000). *Creative collaboration*, New York: Oxford University Press.

Kastenbaum, R., & Aisenberg, R. (1972). *The psychology of death*. New York: Springer.

Kaufman, A., & Kaufman, N. (1983). *Kaufman assessment battery for children: Administration and scoring manual.* Circle Pines, MN: American Guidance Service.

Kerouac, J. (1950). *The town and the city.* New York: Harcourt Brace.

Kerouac, J. (1976). *On the road.* New York: Penguin Books.

Kerouac, J. (1981). *Big Sur.* New York: Penguin Books.

Kerouac, J. (1987). *Dr. Sax.* New York: Grove Press.

Kerouac, J. (1988). *Dharma bums.* New York: Penguin Books.

Kerouac, J. (1991). *Visions of Gerard.* New York: Penguin Books.

Kerouac, J. (1993). *Visions of Cody.* New York: Penguin Books.

Kerouac, J. (1994). *Vanity of Duluoz.* New York: Penguin Books.

Klass, D., Silverman, P. R., & Nickman, S. L. (1996). *Continuing bonds: New understanding of grief.* Washington, DC: Taylor and Francis.

Kohut, H. (1959). Introspection, empathy, and psychoanalysis. *Journal of the American Psychoanalytical Association, 7,* 459-483.

Krueger, D. W. (1983). Childhood parent loss: Developmental impact and adult psychopathology. *American Journal of Psychotherapy, 37*(4), 582-595.

Langbaum, R. (1964). *The gayety of vision.* New York: Random House.

Lasson, F., & Svendsen, C. (1970). *The life and destiny of Isak Dinesen.* New York: Random House.

MacKail, D. (1941). *Story of J. M. B.* London: Peter Davies.

Malinak, D., Hoyt, M., & Patterson, V. (1979). Reaction to the death of a parent in adult life. *American Journal of Psychiatry, 136,* 1152-1156.

Markham, B. (1983). *West with the night.* San Francisco: North Point Press.

Marlow, H., & Wagner, M. (1991). Expression of negative and positive events through writing: Implications for psychotherapy. *Psychology and Health, 14*(2), 193-215.

Martin, M., & Williams, R. (1990). Imagery and emotion: Clinical and experimental approaches. In D. E. Hampson, D. Marks, & T. E. Richardson (Eds.), *Imagery: Current Developments.* London: Routledge.

Morrison, D. (1999). Jack Kerouac: The pulse of memory. In J. Singer & P. Salovey (Eds.), *At play in the fields of consciousness.* Mahwah, NJ: Lawrence Erlbaum.

Morrison, D. (Ed). (1988). *Organizing early experience.* Amityville, NY: Baywood.

Morrison, D., & Mantzicopoulos, Y. (1990). Predicting reading problems at kindergarten for children in second grade: SEARCH as a screen. *Remedial and Special Education, 11*(4), 29-36.

Morrison, D., & Morrison, S. (1988). The development of romantic ideation and J. M. Barries search for the lost boys. In D. Morrison (Ed.), *Organizing early experience.* Amityville, NY: Baywood.

Mullen, E. (1995). *Mullen scale of early learning.* Circle Pines, MN: American Guidance Service.

Nicosia, G. (1994). *Memory babe, a critical biography of Jack Kerouac.* Berkeley CA: University of California Press.

Noam, G. (1988). A constructivists approach to developmental psychopathology. In E. D. Nannis & P. Cowan (Eds.), *Developmental psychopathology and it's treatment.* San Francisco: Jossey-Bass.

Noy, P. (1979). The psychoanalytic theory of cognitive development. *Psychoanalytic Study of the Child, 34,* 169-215.

Piaget, J. (1954). *The construction of reality in the child.* New York: Basic Books.

Piaget, J. (1962). *Play, dreams, and imitation in childhood.* New York: Norton & Company.

Pine, F. (1985). *Developmental theory and clinical process.* New Haven: Yale University Press.

Pollock, G. H. (1962). Childhood parent and sibling loss in adult patients: A comparative study. *Archives of General Psychiatry, 2,* 295-305.

Pollack, G. H. (1978). On siblings, childhood sibling loss, and creativity. *The Annuals of Psychoanalysis, IV,* 443-481.

Rorschach, H. (1942). *Psychodiagnostic: A diagnostic test based on perception.* New York: Grune and Stratton.

Rosengren, K. S., Johnson, C., & P. L. Harris (2000). *Imagining the impossible: Magical, scientific, and religious thinking in children.* Cambridge: Cambridge University Press.

Runco, M., & Richards, R. (1997). *Eminent creativity, everyday creativity, and health.* Greenwich, CT: Ablex Publishing.

Russ, S. (1980). Primary process integration on the Rorschach and achievement in children. *Journal of Personality Assessment, 44,* 338-344.

Russ, S. (1993). *Affect and creativity: The role of affect and play in the creative process.* Hillsdale, NJ: Lawrence Erlbaum.

Russ, S., & Grossman-McKee. (1990). Affective expressions in children's fantasy play, primary process thinking on the Rorschach, and divergent thinking. *Journal of Personality Assessment, 54,* 756-771.

Santostefano, S. (1988). Process and change in child therapy and development: The concept of metaphor. In D. Morrison (Ed.), *Organizing early experience.* Amityville, NY: Baywood.

Schultz, W. T. (1996). An "Orpheus Complex" in two writers of loss. *Biography, 19*(14), 371-393.

Segal, H., Vizueta, N., Biuckians, A., & Pollack, K. (2001-2002). The impact of early experience on the creative process: Findings from a new story completion task. *Imagination, Cognition, and Personality, 2*(21), 91-110.

Silvey, R., & MacKeith, S. (1988). The paracosm: A special form of fantasy. In D. Morrison (Ed.), *Organizing early experience: Imagination and cognition in childhood.* Amityville, NY: Baywood.

Singer, D. (1993). Fantasy and visualization. In C. E. Schaefer (Ed.), *The therapeutic powers of play.* Northvale, NJ: Jason Aronson.

Singer, D., & Singer, J. (1990). *The house of make believe.* Cambridge, MA: Harvard University Press.

Singer, J. (1973). *The child's world of make believe.* New York: Academic Press.

Sparrow, S., Balla, D. A., & Cichetti, D. (1984). *Vineland adaptive behavior scales: Survey form manual.* Circle Pines, MN: American Guidance Service.

Stambrook, M., & Parker, K. (1987). The development of the concept of death in childhood: A review of the literature. *Merrill Palmer Quarterly, 33,* 133-157.

Steinberg, A. (1997). Death as trauma for children: A relational treatment approach. In C. R. Figley, B. Bride, & N. Mazza (Eds.), *Death as trauma: The traumatology of grieving* (pp. 123-137). Washington, DC: Taylor and Francis.

Stern, N. N. (1977). *The first relationship.* Cambridge, MA: Harvard University Press.

Sternberg, R. J. (Ed.) (1999). *Handbook of creativity.* New York: Cambridge University Press.

Taylor, M. (1999). *Imaginary companions and the children who create them*. New York: Oxford University Press.

Thurman, J. (1982). *Isak Dinesen*. New York: St. Martin's Press.

Trzeinski, E. (1977). *Silence will speak*. Chicago: University of Chicago Press.

Vanderberg, B. (1991) Is epistemology enough? An existential consideration of development. *American Psychologist, 46*(12), 1278-1286.

Wadeson, H. (2002). Art therapy and the elephant. *Bulletin of Psychology and the Arts, 2*, 69-73.

Walsh, F., & McGoldrick, M. (Eds.). (1991). *Living beyond loss: Death in the family*. New York: Norton.

Webb, N. B. (2002). *Helping bereaved children*. New York: The Guilford Press.

Wilhelm, H. (1985). *I'll always love you*. New York: Dragonfly Books.

Winnicott, D. (1965). *The maturational process and the facilitating environment*. New York: International Universities Press.

Wordsworth, W. (1805). *The prelude*. E. DeSelincourt (Ed.). New York: Oxford University Press.

Yalom, I. (1980). *Exisential psychotherapy*. New York: Basic Books.

Young, L., & Fast, I. (1985). Omnipotence and primary creativity in Rorschach responses. In I. Fast (Ed.), *Event theory*. Hillsdale, NJ: Lawrence Erlbaum.

Zimmer, H. (1973). *The king and the corpse*. Princeton: Princeton University Press.

Index